GAMBLING ADDICTION IN IRELAND

CAUSES, CONSEQUENCES AND RECOVERY

COLIN O'GARA

VERITAS

Published 2019 by
Veritas Publications
7–8 Lower Abbey Street
Dublin 1, Ireland
publications@veritas.ie
www.veritas.ie

ISBN 978 1 84730 886 3

10 9 8 7 6 5 4 3 2 1

Designed by Pádraig McCormack, Veritas Publications
Printed in Ireland by Fineprint Ltd, Dublin

Case studies within this book are entirely fictional. They are representative of common presentations to addiction services for problem gambling treatment. Any identifying details such as names, age, gender, background details, occupation, interests, addictive behaviours and family members have all been changed in order to avoid any possible resemblance to actual cases.

For individuals and families
struggling with gambling disorder

CONTENTS

FOREWORD
DR MARK GRIFFITHS   13

ACKNOWLEDGEMENTS   17

ABOUT THE AUTHOR   19

INTRODUCTION   23

CAUSES

CHAPTER ONE
WHAT MAKES A GAMBLER BECOME ADDICTED?   31

CONSEQUENCES

CHAPTER TWO
SYMPTOMS, HARM AND DIAGNOSIS   49

CHAPTER THREE
MENTAL HEALTH AND GAMBLING DISORDER   71

RECOVERY

CHAPTER FOUR
TREATMENT AND STAGES OF CHANGE   89

CHAPTER FIVE
MUTUAL SUPPORT FOR GAMBLING DISORDER   111

CHAPTER SIX
SELF-HELP STRATEGIES   129

CHAPTER SEVEN
SPECIALIST HELP IN THE OUTPATIENT SETTING   153

CHAPTER EIGHT
INPATIENT TREATMENT   173

USEFUL CONTACTS   187

SELF-ASSESSMENT AND HELPSHEETS

Self-Assessment: Gambling Questionnaire   69

Questions to consider if you are worried
about a family member's gambling   81

Tackling a potential gambling problem
with a family member in a non-confrontational way   83

Dealing with debt as a result of gambling addiction 109

Action plan for an individual
affected by gambling disorder   169

Action plan for family members of an
individual affected by gambling disorder   170

FOREWORD

I was delighted to be asked by Professor Colin O'Gara
to write the foreword of his book on gambling
addiction in Ireland. Over the last few years I worked
closely with Colin on a number of research papers
about the gambling situation in Ireland and I have
learned many things from him. Professor O'Gara
is as passionate about wanting to educate citizens
in Ireland concerning problem gambling in his own
country as much as I do here in the United Kingdom.
Dissemination is an important aspect for anyone who
works in the gambling studies field simply because
there are so many different stakeholders when it
comes to this particular topic.

In 1987 I began a PhD on slot-machine gambling
and little did I know at the time that I would still be
as interested in the psychology of gambling over three
decades later. The academic study of gambling has
come a long way in the past three decades. All around
the world, gambling has become more destigmatised

and more demasculinised. The rise of the internet has brought new ways to gamble and even bigger challenges in terms of player protection, harm-minimisation, social responsibility, and responsible gambling. Put in the simplest of ways, anyone with a smartphone is walking around with a casino or bookmaker in their back pocket or handbag.

People's attitudes to gambling have softened and gambling is now seen as a socially acceptable leisure activity rather than a sin or a vice. Continued legislative deregulation all around the world will almost certainly lead to more opportunities and access to gambling than we have ever seen before. The downside of deregulation is that more people will gamble. As a consequence, there will be a growing number of gambling 'casualties' – some of whom will want professional intervention and treatment – and this is one of the central themes running through Professor O'Gara's book. Protection of vulnerable and susceptible individuals from gambling is one of the main reasons that we need regulation and legislation.

Gambling is multifaceted and many factors may come into play in various ways and at different levels. They may be biological, social or psychological. No single level of analysis is sufficient to explain gambling behaviour. Individuals are self-determining agents. Examining gambling and problem gambling as biopsychosocial behaviour makes it evident that individual differences and broader contextual factors must all be considered. Moreover, it indicates that a variety of treatments, from a variety of standpoints, could be beneficial simultaneously. A narrow focus upon one theoretical perspective cannot be justified in understanding problem gambling, nor in treating it. Professor O'Gara's book provides an excellent 'one-stop shop' for the casual or interested reader to learn about some of these perspectives.

Over the last few decades, I have been relentless in trying to get gambling issues on many agendas, including those in the mental health and legal arenas. And I know Professor O'Gara has tried to do the same in Ireland – a country where there is very little research on the topic. Back in 2009, I co-edited a book, with Dr Gerhard Meyer and Dr Tobias Hayer, on problem gambling in Europe with chapters written about gambling in almost every European country. However, Ireland was not represented as no one at the time was doing any research on gambling in Ireland. If we ever edit a second edition of that book, we will surely be asking Professor O'Gara to write that chapter for us!

I have argued for many years that gambling in its most excessive forms can be just as destructive as any other form of addictive behaviour for the individual and that appropriate regulation and legislation needs to be put in place. Obviously Professor O'Gara's book was not written to highlight my own areas of research or concern, but the gambling agenda in Ireland is having a psychosocial impact on many individuals including those who already gamble and those who may be initiated through the increased gambling opportunities that will become available via new forms of technology.

I very much hope that this book will become the first port of call for anyone working with or wanting to know about problem gambling in Ireland. I wish Professor O'Gara every success with the book and hope that readers will find it a stimulating and educational read. I also hope that you, the reader, will feed back your own experiences and thoughts back to Professor O'Gara directly about the important issues he has raised.

Dr Mark Griffiths
Distinguished Professor of Behavioural Addiction
International Gaming Research Unit
Psychology Department
Nottingham Trent University
United Kingdom

May 2019

ACKNOWLEDGEMENTS

I wish to acknowledge the courage, determination and humanity of the patients and families I have met in the course of treating gambling disorder.

Donna Doherty, Commissioning Editor of Veritas proposed this book and gave astute input and guidance throughout its development. Daragh Reddin, Manager of Publications at Veritas, also gave excellent feedback on the development of this book.

A big thank you to all my colleagues at St John of God Hospital, especially my clinical and research team for their dedication to addiction treatment.

ABOUT THE AUTHOR

I was appointed consultant psychiatrist and head of addiction services at St John of God Hospital in 2007. After graduating from medical school in Cork in 1999, I trained as a senior house officer and specialist registrar in psychiatry on the Maudsley Hospital training schemes in London. In addition to training in general adult psychiatry, I also trained in addiction at the National Addiction Centre, Institute of Psychiatry, London. This included training with many world leaders in the area of addiction medicine. During the course of this clinical training I was awarded a competitive research training grant to study the genetics of cocaine addiction. This was my first period of working in addiction genetics and lead to an interest in pursuing a PhD in genetics. I was awarded membership of the Royal College of Psychiatrists (the professional body of psychiatrists in the UK) in 2003. I have conducted research in many areas of addiction here in Ireland and at the Institute of Psychiatry in

London. My work features in international scientific journals, medical publications, media articles and books. I head up a research group at St John of God Hospital within the School of Medicine at UCD. Current areas of investigation are gambling-service provision, gambling stigma, responsible gambling initiatives, over-the-counter pill addiction and optimising efficacy of both inpatient and outpatient alcohol addiction rehabilitation. I was awarded a PhD from the University of London/Kings for work on the genetics of nicotine addiction in 2010. I regularly tutor medical students and other health professionals.

Within UCD, I was appointed clinical professor at the School of Medicine in 2018 after holding previous academic appointments of senior clinical lecturer and associate clinical professor. I worked with the UK charity Action on Addiction and regularly interact with the public, media and expert audiences. These interactions provide an opportunity to promote holistic, non-shame-based treatment for addiction and also reduce stigma associated with addiction and mental health. In recent years, with others, I have called for a regulatory framework and funding of treatment services for gambling disorder in Ireland.

I work full time in clinical services, treating gambling disorder on a daily basis. This entails working with individuals and families at their most vulnerable. It is a privilege to work with so many courageous and inspiring individuals as they make their journey out of the misery of gambling addiction.

Sadly, we don't assist everyone to long-term recovery, but in the many cases that we do, it is highly rewarding and satisfying to observe people gain control over the illness. Recovery from gambling disorder can sometimes seem like an impossible goal for many individuals. To witness the huge changes that people *can* make from the depths of this addiction to recovery is inspiring.

INTRODUCTION

I began working in my current role as a consultant psychiatrist and head of addiction services at St John of God Hospital in January 2007. Since then, I have encountered dramatic changes in gambling addiction presentations to our service. In the early days of treating gambling addiction, the problem was almost exclusively related to gambling that took place in betting shops. Gradually, over the years, we encountered an increase in online problems to the point nowadays where online gambling is almost always a feature of this addiction.

The rapid development of smartphone technology and online gambling software has made gambling more accessible than ever before. In addition, successive governments still struggle to implement a regulatory framework for gambling. All of these developments have conspired to create an environment where some individuals can be seriously harmed by gambling and I have witnessed the intense pain and suffering of those affected by gambling addiction.

Gambling is also emerging in the internet gaming industry. Children are being exposed to video games where there are gambling features. Opportunities to win coveted resources within video games are sometimes made available to players through the spin of a wheel. These 'loot boxes' have been criticised at home and abroad as a form of grooming, whereby children are introduced to the basics of gambling at a very early age. As with gambling itself, the political response to the problem is inadequate.

Irish individuals, families, spouses and children are suffering as a result of problem gambling. Simon Stevens, the chief executive of the NHS in the UK, told a recent conference that gambling addiction is one of the 'new threats to health'. Although problem gambling affects Irish women, it appears that young Irish men are especially vulnerable, with sports betting being a particularly enticing option for male gamblers. It is hardly surprising given that nearly 60 per cent of the teams in the top two divisions of the English Premier League had gambling companies sponsor their shirts at the start of the 2018/2019 season. Any reasonable analysis of the use of advertising and sponsorship in the English premiership and championship leagues would have to conclude that gambling is being normalised. It is common practice for young Irish men to spend Saturday afternoons watching and gambling on sport, be it in betting shops or with recourse to their phone or computer. Unfortunately, we do not have statistics on this matter due to a serious lack of research in that area. Our own research group in St John of God's is conducting as many studies in problem gambling as we can but much more research in Ireland is required.

This brings me to the main reason for writing this book: raising awareness is the first step in persuading policymakers and fundholders to create treatment services and research facilities to tackle the problem. I hope that in writing this book, I am not only providing help for those directly affected by the issue, but encouraging those in power to give gambling addiction the priority it deserves.

I was also anxious to collate the important information that was needed for individuals and families affected by gambling addiction in Ireland and so, in Chapter One, I discuss the societal and personal factors which influence gambling addiction. In Chapter Two, I offer help in identifying the symptoms of problem gambling, explain how it is diagnosed, and discuss the serious impact of this illness on individuals and their families. Within this chapter, I use case studies that describe the different categories of severity surrounding gambling disorder, ranging from mild to severe. In Chapter Three, I highlight the fact that gambling addiction is a serious mental illness which can co-exist alongside other mental health issues explored here.

For years I have been troubled by the fact that there was not a single source of information in relation to gambling addiction treatment in Ireland. Therefore, collecting the most important information in book form for the benefit of the general reader seemed like the obvious solution. Gambling addiction usually presents in a painful fashion. As the illness is frequently hidden for months or even years, when it does emerge, it is often in a particularly disruptive and stressful fashion, causing great pain for both the patient and his or her loved ones. Lies, deceit and manipulation leave relatives and the individual at loggerheads. Relatives often have no idea of what to do or where to turn. In the majority of first meetings I have with patients and their families, their knowledge of how to proceed is poor. Consequently, in this book I have concentrated heavily on providing information that I hope will assist individuals and families on their journey to reconciliation and recovery.

Chapter Four introduces the stages of addiction recovery, while the subsequent chapter examines mutual support for gambling disorder recovery, outlining the benefits of Gamblers Anonymous, Gam-Anon and alternative approaches also available to the patient.

Chapter Six identifies self-help strategies to overcome problem gambling, while Chapter Seven outlines the process of recovery in an outpatient setting. The final chapter considers the inpatient experience and concludes with a section entitled 'After the Inpatient Programme and Beyond', wherein the many positive changes that occur with long-term abstinence are explored.

Throughout this book I have tried to report on the amazing recoveries from gambling disorder that I experience on a daily basis. It is critical for individuals and families to understand that recovery is possible, in even the most apparently hopeless of situations. Yes, it is true that some do not recover or take a very long time to recover. Thankfully, these are in the minority. The process of recovery can be painful, stressful and frustrating for all involved. When a loved one is not getting well, families can blame the patient, each other, clinical services or individual team members. A sense of hopelessness can creep in, along with a belief that 'they'll never get well'. As this book explains, patients *do* get well, sometimes after years of suffering, and they go on to live successful and fulfilling lives. Gambling disorders can also have a detrimental effect on family relationships, but the good news again is that, following a process of reconciliation and healing, they usually recover over time.

CAUSES

CHAPTER ONE
WHAT MAKES A GAMBLER BECOME ADDICTED?

For those of us working in clinical services, the past decade has seen a distinct increase in the numbers presenting for the treatment of problem gambling. Gambling problems are not restricted to a particular age group in Ireland and issues can emerge at any stage of life. Many of the individuals we treat for problem gambling report the onset of problems in adolescence. Others develop problems in middle age. Very rarely, older people suffering from Parkinson's disease or restless leg syndrome are prescribed medication that can, as a side effect, cause problem gambling. The severity of the problem also varies from mild through to severe (see Chapter Two). Gambling problems arise because gambling is essentially an addictive behaviour. It is, of course, the case that a large majority of the population can gamble without a problem. A minority, however, will develop very serious and debilitating problems as a result, so it is important to consider some of the factors that influence this.

Biological influences

A simple risk factor associated with gambling disorder is being male. Other accumulated scientific evidence revealing the underlying brain abnormalities in gambling disorder has been published in recent years.

- An advanced form of MRI scanning called functional magnetic resonance imaging (FMRI) demonstrated abnormalities in an area of the brain called the ventromedial prefrontal cortex. Functional MRI scans usually involve the subject taking part in a gambling task, i.e. a gambling game while in an MRI scanner. Various compounds called ligands can also be injected into the subject so that areas of the brain are more likely to be highlighted when the scan takes place. The prefrontal cortex is the area of the brain thought to be critical in risk processing, which is very important in gambling. Problem gambling is characterised by a whole host of impaired thinking strategies sometimes referred to as cognitive distortions. These distortions are most likely mediated by abnormalities in the ventromedial prefrontal cortex.

- Various neuropsychological studies show that if you suffer from faulty risk evaluation (due to the brain abnormalities outlined above), you are more likely to persist with destructive gambling. Neuropsychological tests are performed by psychologists or psychiatrists trained to carry out detailed assessments of brain function. These tests consist of usually quite lengthy questionnaires and tests that reveal deficits in specific brain areas. Multiple neuropsychological studies have demonstrated deficits in key areas such as the ventromedial prefrontal cortex. These findings are particularly important as they converge with the MRI studies and point strongly to gambling disorder as an addiction brain disorder with very specific deficits.

- A growing literature suggests that genetics play a key role in the development of gambling disorder. Studies indicate that genes contribute approximately 50 per cent of the variation of liability for disordered gambling. Dopamine is a chemical released by nerve and brain cells responsible for mediating reward. When we experience a very happy event, dopamine is released in nerve and brain cells. Dopamine is also released while eating and during sexual activity. It is our body's way of telling us that the process we are engaging in is good for us.

In gambling disorder, the dopamine-rich reward centres are dysfunctional. The patient loses control over gambling and lacks an ability to judge risk in a normal way. Several genes in the dopamine system have been highlighted as candidates for contributing to dysfunction in brain reward areas like the ventromedial prefontal cortex. Studies of cases (those affected by gambling disorder) and controls (those not affected by gambling disorder) demonstrate statistically significant associations between certain dopamine gene variations (polymorphisms) and cases. This type of study is called a genetic association study and ideally contains thousands of cases and controls. The larger the study size, the more accurate the data that emerges.

Environmental contributors

Factors outside of genetics have also proven to be important in the genesis of gambling disorder. These non-genetic factors are often called psychosocial or environmental factors. Parental gambling is associated with higher rates of gambling initiation in offspring and also higher levels of problem gambling in adolescents. Family members often introduce young members to gambling and there can be an acceptance and even promotion of gambling 'skills' within some families. Commencement of gambling at a young age, divorce, poor parental supervision, being widowed or separated are all associated with problem gambling. So too is a lower socioeconomic status. A personal history of childhood neglect or trauma, as well as being associated with a host of psychiatric problems, is also associated with problem gambling. The trauma reported in many studies over many years includes physical and sexual abuse, life-threatening illness, parental death and parental mental illness.

International studies demonstrate the importance of availability and density of gambling and the development of gambling problems. The lack of gambling regulation appears to be a major contributor to the availability and density of gambling products in Ireland. All, including the gambling industry, appear to be calling for regulation but no substantial advances, if any, are being made. The Gambling Control Bill draft of 2013 promised funding for treatment services and research. To date, very little of taxed gambling revenues has been used for the setting up of problem gambling services, including research facilities. Most forms of gambling are readily available in Ireland, with our own research data suggesting that sports betting is the most common form of gambling. Online gambling, casino games and poker are often considered more harmful than other forms of gambling; football pools, bingo and National Lottery are perceived as less harmful. Electronic gaming machines, also known as fixed odds betting terminals, are thankfully not available in Ireland. This type of electronic slot machine is commonplace in the United Kingdom, and is dubbed the 'crack cocaine of gambling' due to its promotion of high stakes and high pace gambling. Studies from the United States suggest that men have a preference for gambling products where there is a competitive component, whereas women prefer gambling against a house or a monotonous form of gambling like slot machines. Men generally gamble more than women and are more prone to gamble with products that are more likely to cause gambling harm.

Defining the scale of the problem in Ireland is difficult. There have been no large-scale prevalence surveys conducted here to date to give us an idea as to the extent of the problem. In fact, there is very little research at all conducted on problem gambling in Ireland. Our research group, one of the only Irish groups researching problem gambling, conducted the National Online Gambling Survey, which was published in late 2017 in the *Irish Journal of Psychological Medicine*. This was the first piece of research conducted on a sample of its size (over two hundred problem gamblers) in Ireland. The results of our study confirmed what we were observing in our clinics. Most of our sample demonstrated a range of problem gambling features. Three quarters of our sample had borrowed or sold something to get money to gamble. We also found that a similar number of respondents stated that gambling had caused financial problems for them and their household. In the absence of large-scale prevalence surveys on disordered gambling in Ireland, one has to make do with data from the UK and extrapolate for the Irish situation. Data from the British Gambling Prevalence Survey and Gambling Commission surveys indicate that gambling disorder affects up to 5 per cent of the UK population, with close to 1 per cent severely affected. Assuming similar rates in Ireland, this would suggest at least forty thousand individuals are severely affected by this illness. Up to two hundred and fifty thousand are likely to be affected to a lesser degree by mild to moderate gambling disorder (see Chapter Two). By any standards, this suggests that there are many Irish people affected by problem gambling. International data suggest that very few (only about one in ten) of those affected by severe problem gambling receive treatment. To compound matters, anywhere up to half of the people that do get into treatment will drop out. This suggests that many Irish people are suffering in silence.

Availability of gambling in Ireland

A decade ago, referrals to our treatment service for problem gambling were almost entirely bookmaker-based gambling problems. Occasionally, we treated addiction to stock and share trading but internet-based problems were relatively sparse. All this has changed with the intensive development of online gambling products. Ireland has experienced huge increases in the availability of online gambling facilities. Smartphone usage has exploded with the figures increasing year on year. Online gambling presents a particular worry as it offers permanent availability, anonymity and increased speed of play. The ability to gamble from the comfort of your own home is frequently cited as a reason to gamble online. Our treatment facility regularly encounters gambling histories whereby the individual gambled almost entirely in secret within the home, in bedrooms, gardens, attics, toilets, and at the dinner table. This is what online gambling has created – a full suite of gambling products available 24/7 without the user even having to leave the house.

The 'always on' nature of online gambling, combined with the ease of betting, contributes to online gambling being more addictive than conventional gambling. This is particularly the case for young gamblers. The rapid pace of technological advances is also a major concern. Personal devices, in particular the smartphone, are becoming ever more powerful and sophisticated. Nowadays there are also myriad reasons why people use a phone or appear distracted on a phone – work, emails, social media, hobbies, WhatsApp groups. These activities are often used as excuses for extended use of a phone while the individual is in fact gambling.

Problem gambling is the continuation of gambling in the face of adverse consequences. Participants engaging in two or more activities online, or in certain activities such as live action sports betting or poker, are more likely to be problem gamblers. Also, participants owning multiple online accounts present with higher rates of gambling problems. This data supports the concept that the online space is dangerous when it comes to the development of gambling problems. Although online players can currently use facilities to limit the amount they bet, this is on a voluntary basis. I and others have called for the introduction of mandatory limit setting in Ireland, whereby online players would have to indicate the maximum amount they wished to bet, spend and lose during a specified time period. If these parameters were exceeded, the account would be automatically shut down for an agreed period of time.

Gambling advertising

Another important environmental factor in the causation of gambling addiction is gambling advertising. Gambling advertising has also become vastly more prevalent in recent years. It is nearly impossible to watch sporting events now without encountering gambling adverts. Many in Ireland suggest that gambling has become 'normalised' through incessant high-profile advertising and sponsorship of sporting events. Children continue to be exposed to hundreds, if not thousands, of gambling adverts every year. Without Irish data on the subject we need to look once again to our neighbours in the UK for an approximation as to what the levels of advertising might be. Data from Ofcom, the UK communications regulator, is damning. Although now somewhat dated, the period of study from 2007–2012 showed gambling adverts had increased from two hundred and thirty-four thousand to 1.4 million. The Gambling Act 2005 in the UK opened the door to TV advertising of sports betting, poker and online casinos. This deregulation of the sector came into force in 2007. Prior legislation only allowed advertising of the National Lottery, football pools and bingo premises. The most shocking data from Ofcom is the revelation that in 2012 television viewers were exposed to a total of 1.4 million gambling adverts in a year, with those under sixteen each exposed to two hundred and eleven a year. One can only assume that the current situation in Ireland regarding gambling advertising is the same or worse since 2012.

Stewart Kenny, the co-founder of Paddy Power in Ireland, has recently (2018) called for a reduction in the number of adverts made available, suggesting that the level of advertising in Ireland was 'normalising' gambling for children in particular. The international research literature supports Mr Kenny's views, with studies demonstrating that gambling advertising increases public acceptance. Studies also agree that gambling advertising in sport normalises gambling for children and adolescents. Some research on adolescent gambling behaviour suggests that adolescents are actually prompted to gamble having been exposed to adverts. This mirrors research from tobacco and alcohol advertising, whereby advertising has a strong impact on young people taking up the practices, maintaining the behaviours, and on remaining loyal to particular brands. The sophistication and complexity of gambling advertising in Ireland has also increased quite dramatically. The past decade has seen the arrival of high-profile celebrities fronting promotions for sports betting.

The use of 'embedded' adverts, or those shown during live events, has also increased. These adverts may be more detrimental to problem gamblers than to the general population. Live odds or 'in play' betting has become the fashionable way for young men in particular to spend a Saturday afternoon (e.g. 'Ronaldo to score a hattrick 8/1' or 'Paul Pogba to score first 4/1'). Advertising is focused on promoting the bets and gambling behaviours that net the gambling provider the most profit. Phillip Newall, at the University of Stirling in Scotland, describes the increasing complexity of gambling products in recent years ('How bookies make your money', *Judgment and Decision Making*, 10:3, May 2015, pp. 225–31). He outlines simple three-outcome bets between two teams: Team A wins; a draw; Team B wins. He also outlines more complex bets; for example, forecasting the first goalscorer (at least twenty players could score the first goal) or the final match scoreline (an indefinite but large number, e.g. Team A wins 4-3). Newall has demonstrated in his research on bookmaker behaviour that complex bets during the 2014 soccer World Cup were much more profitable than simple three-outcome bets. The concern at present is that adverts for complex bets may have a disproportionately negative effect on problem gamblers. This is worrying, as current gambling advertising in Ireland and elsewhere appears to be concentrated on complex bets.

Service provision

Poor service provision for gambling disorder in Ireland aggravates the situation by allowing the problem to fester. Our research team investigated service provision in Ireland in a research study published in the *International Journal of Mental Health and Addiction* in 2018. We found that there are varying levels of input throughout the country but these inputs are largely uncoordinated and do not prioritise problem gambling alone. This means that the person suffering from gambling disorder, more often than not, will have difficulty accessing services in Ireland. It also means that one may have to navigate generic addiction services to find help with gambling problems. It is clear that many community addiction teams (CATs) are doing their best to provide gambling services within existing addiction treatment services. The problem is that gambling disorder treatment requires dedicated specialist resources. Existing addiction services are already stretched. This leaves the prospect of very little actual structured help for gambling disorder on the ground at present. The numbers presenting for gambling disorder treatment may have something to do with this.

As we have seen, only 10 per cent of individuals suffering from severe gambling disorder are thought to present for treatment. Without a critical mass of individuals presenting for treatment, it is unlikely that service commissioners will make gambling disorder a priority.

SUMMARY

- Although we do not know the prevalence of problem gambling in Ireland, we can approximate from international data. This data would suggest that the scale of the problem in Ireland is far from insignificant, with perhaps a quarter of a million Irish people affected. Legislation governing the regulation of gambling in Ireland is greatly outdated at present. Service provision is patchy at best. If one requires help for gambling disorder in Ireland, accessing services will often be problematic.

- Online gambling has dramatically changed the face of gambling in Ireland. Online gambling's 'always on' nature, combined with the rapid development of betting products, has led to the creation of more addictive forms of gambling. Problem online gambling can be very hidden and may be more dangerous for younger players in terms of addiction.

- Gambling advertising is widespread in Ireland. Adverts are increasingly focused on complex bets and live odds features, where there is a greater return for the gambling provider. Live odds betting is increasingly the choice of young men for recreation. Research demonstrates that gambling adverts normalise gambling within adolescent groups and actually prompt young people to gamble. Gambling adverts present a challenge for those in recovery as they act as continuous cues and triggers for relapse.

CONSEQUENCES

CHAPTER TWO

SYMPTOMS, HARM AND DIAGNOSIS

Although the term 'problem gambling' is used frequently, it is not actually used in clinical services to define gambling problems. In the United States the term 'gambling disorder' is used. The European classificatory system for addiction problems released by the World Health Organization, called the *International Classification of Diseases* (ICD-10), describes a disorder of 'pathological gambling'.

In May 2013, gambling problems were reclassified as 'gambling disorder' in the American Psychiatric Association's book of psychiatric and addiction disorders, the *Diagnostic and Statistical Manual of Mental Disorders* (DSM-5). This is the text used by psychiatrists to diagnose gambling problems and allows psychiatrists to classify gambling problems in an agreed and coherent fashion. Prior to the reclassification of gambling problems as 'gambling disorder', gambling problems were not considered to be addiction problems. They were thought to fit less with addictions and more with a category called 'impulse control disorders', which includes problems such as pyromania. A significant body of research was conducted on gambling problems since the previous edition of the DSM (DSM-4). Thousands of inputs from clinicians and scientists around the world working with gambling problems were collated. In addition, an expert committee examined the possible reclassification of gambling problems. The DSM-5 committee reclassified gambling problems because all of the data collated from around the world indicated that the features of gambling addiction are essentially the same as alcohol and drug addiction.

Although there is no alcohol or chemical substance ingested in the case of gambling disorder, the conditions otherwise present in a remarkably similar way. Gambling disorder is characterised by a need to gamble more in order to maintain the same desired effect or 'high'. Alcohol and drug addiction are characterised by a need to take increasing amounts of a substance to maintain the same desired effect. As with alcohol and drug addiction, gambling disorder is also characterised by withdrawal symptoms such as irritability and craving. Tolerance (needing to engage in increasing instances of the activity for it to have the same desired effect), irritability on cutting down, repeated unsuccessful efforts to control the behaviour, preoccupation with the behaviour, distress, lies, loss of relationships, loss of occupation, loss of opportunities and relying on others to relieve financial distress are all clinical features that are equally prominent in gambling disorder as they are in alcohol and substance addiction.

In addition, gambling disorder and substance addictions share similar psychiatric co-morbidities (co-occuring disorders). Elevated rates of co-occurring psychiatric and addiction problems are found in gambling disorder. The best available research at present indicates the highest rate of co-occurring conditions with gambling disorder are nicotine dependence (60 per cent), followed by substance use disorder (58 per cent), any type of mood disorder (38 per cent) and any type of anxiety disorder (37 per cent). Furthermore, gambling disorder, like alcohol and drug addiction, attracts considerable public stigma.

Identifying a problem

Problem gambling presents with a range of consequences to the individual and the people around them. The following are signs and symptoms of gambling disorder, some of which can cause significant harm over time.

- **Being overly preoccupied with gambling:** This can involve thinking about odds, planning the next gambling session, ruminating over past losses, reliving past wins and fantasising about vast riches as a result of gambling. Early on, problem gamblers talk openly about their interest in gambling; however, in the latter stages of problem gambling, individuals often hide their interest and gambling behaviour. Preoccupation can be observed through a change of behaviour. Problem gamblers may appear aloof, detached and distracted. Families will speak of a change in the personality of their loved one (from outgoing and bubbly to quiet and introverted). Problem gamblers who have been in treatment for some time may learn to hide their preoccupation by pretending that everything is alright and feigning good humour. Many of those in recovery speak of the effort involved in presenting themselves as normal to the world, when in reality they are suffering with intense preoccupation around gambling activities.

- **Chasing losses:** Within the mind of the problem gambler, there is always a way out of a previous loss by chasing losses. This is one of the features of problem gambling that makes it so harmful in comparison to other addictive behaviours: chasing losses can incur massive financial difficulties as the problem gambler continues to spend any available funds in the belief that they are due a 'big win'. As we have seen, various studies indicate that the brain is malfunctioning during this process. The assessment of risk is impaired in problem gamblers, whereby they make poor decisions around the continuation of gambling during a run of losses. A recreational gambler will be able to walk away from a series of losses, whereas a problem gambler will continue to gamble in the belief that a series of losses will lead to a win.

- **Gambling with larger amounts of money:** This can sometimes be a tell-tale sign that something is wrong. A pattern of increasing time spent gambling can also be a worrying feature. It is not uncommon for a problem gambler to spend an entire month's wages in a few hours. Problem gamblers frequently underestimate the amount they spend on gambling. If you are concerned about your own gambling, simply calculating the amount spent over a day, week and month can be a good starting point in working out whether there is a problem or not.

- **Changes in behaviour:** Family members sometimes notice that there is a change in behaviour as the gambling of their loved one becomes more problematic. It may simply be that the normal routine of the person changes as problem gambling kicks in. They can report their loved one becoming moodier, angry and distant. Other reports are that there is an increase in snappiness, irritability or agitation.

- **Borrowing money or selling items to fund gambling:** Our recent research of online gamblers in Ireland showed that three quarters of our study sample had borrowed money or sold something to fund their gambling. This is a clear warning sign with regard to problem gambling. Problem gamblers are often careful to avoid detection, borrowing from different people and telling lies regarding the need for the money. Selling items where there is no clear reason to do so sometimes raises concern about a potential problem. Similarly, family members often talk about not questioning certain behaviours of their loved one when they feel that they should have in retrospect. Families can be distressed that they didn't pursue something that they were suspicious about at the time.

- **Evidence of problem gambling around the home:** Bank account statements may show evidence of excessive gambling. Sometimes getting access to bank statements can be difficult as the person suffering from problem gambling may seek to keep all mail and bills from their partner or loved ones in order to hide a problem.

- **Excessive time on a smartphone:** There are many reasons nowadays why people spend too much time on a smartphone – social media, news sites, video gaming, work emails. Excessive gambling is another reason for excessive smartphone usage. Family members of a problem gambler often recount that they had no idea that there was any problem apart from their loved one spending a great deal of time on the smartphone. As gambling disorder is often a hidden illness, this may be the only clue for family members that there may be a problem with gambling.

- **Failed attempts to reduce gambling:** Many problem gamblers are aware that they should gamble less, but when they attempt to do so encounter a dip in mood, with increased irritability or restlessness. If a person continues to experience urges or cravings to gamble when there are clear problems (debt, relationship and work setbacks), this can indicate addiction.

- **Lack of insight:** Most individuals suffering from addiction struggle to see the extent of their problem. Gambling disorder can be particularly problematic in this regard. We encounter individuals who have clearly experienced grave issues as a result of gambling but remain convinced that they will have a 'big win' to solve all their problems.

- **Gambling to regulate emotions:** Gambling regularly to distract from low moods or anxiety may be a sign that gambling is being used to drown out emotions rather than to deal with them in a healthy manner, i.e. exercise, talking to friends and family, or counselling.

- **Lying is very common in all addiction illnesses:** Gambling disorder is no different. If you are lying to loved ones about the extent or nature of your gambling, this is likely to indicate a problem.

- **Absenteeism:** Problem gambling can result in late nights and an overall lack of self-care. As the illness progresses it can lead to a disregard for other interests in life, such as career development. This can be evident in an altered work pattern and an increase in the number of sick days taken.

- **Losing friends or having arguments with loved ones:** Conflict is an inevitable component of problem gambling when loved ones challenge the behaviours of the individual. As the insight of the individual is often poor, they can believe that their loved ones are overly critical or merely seeking attention.

Making a diagnosis

Gambling problems are not all of the same severity, presenting on a spectrum of harm from mild through to severe. Clinicians use the following classificatory system from the American Psychiatric Association's *Diagnostic and Statistical Manual of Mental Disorders* (DSM-5) to assess the level of the illness:

A. Persistent and recurrent problematic gambling behaviour leading to clinically significant impairment or distress, as indicated by the individual exhibiting four (or more) of the following in a twelve-month period:

1. Needs to gamble with increasing amounts of money in order to achieve the desired excitement.

2. Is restless or irritable when attempting to cut down or stop gambling.

3. Has made repeated unsuccessful efforts to control, cut back, or stop gambling.

4. Is often preoccupied with gambling (e.g. having persistent thoughts of reliving past gambling experiences, handicapping or planning the next venture, thinking of ways to get money with which to gamble).

5. Often gambles when feeling distressed (e.g. helpless, guilty, anxious, depressed).

6. After losing money by gambling, often returns another day to get even ('chasing' one's losses).

7. Lies to conceal the extent of involvement with gambling.
8. Has jeopardised or lost a significant relationship, job, educational or career opportunity because of gambling.
9. Relies on others to provide money to relieve desperate financial situations caused by gambling.

B. The gambling behaviour is not better explained by a manic episode.

Mania (a manic episode) is abnormality of mood whereby the mood is greatly elevated from baseline. When mood is elevated, behaviours such as overspending and gambling can arise. As these difficulties arise as a direct result of mania, they are not classified as gambling disorder difficulties.

Gambling disorder and the spectrum of harm

Population prevalence figures quoted for problem gambling often reflect the severe end of the illness, rather than the full spectrum of harm associated with problem gambling. The following case studies outline the different severities of gambling disorder. We will focus first on the case of Pat, who presents with gambling disorder of mild intensity.

CASE STUDY
Gambling disorder of mild intensity

Pat, a twenty-one-year-old student, loves sport. As a child, he excelled at both GAA and rugby. He was happy at school and had many friends. He was very pleased with four hundred points in the Leaving Cert and was delighted to get his first CAO choice of Arts. He started playing football with his university team and excelled here too until a bad injury sidelined him for the best part of a year. Pat's normal routine was turned on its head.

Without regular training, Pat suddenly had a lot of time on his hands. Alcohol use increased on nights out. Pat's peer group, especially his inner circle, enjoy gambling on major sporting events. Major horse racing meetings, GAA and premiership football matches, tennis, golf, boxing and mixed martial arts events are all popular with Pat and his group of friends when it comes to betting opportunities.

Following his injury, the frequency of Pat's betting increased, as did the amount he was betting. One Saturday he had lost €300 on an accumulator bet. He immediately went to the ATM to take out another €300. He proceeded to bet on a football match and a golf tournament that were also on at the same time. By the time both events had finished, he had also lost this €300.

Chastened by the experience, he attempted to cut down on gambling, but to no avail. Whenever he cut down he noticed that he didn't feel quite right. Those around Pat said that he was snappy and irritable and had lied about the amount of money he had lost. He mentioned these concerns to one of his best friends, Paul.

Paul had a cousin who had suffered a severe gambling problem in the past and suggested that Pat visit his GP for advice. Pat's GP was very supportive, and was able to advise on local GA meetings. His GP was also able to reassure him that he was not depressed but that he was drinking too much and needed to cut down his alcohol intake, which was adversely affecting his judgement and clearly increasing his urge to gamble.

COMMENT

Pat's case demonstrates four DSM-5 criteria. Pat was gambling with increasing amounts in order to achieve the desired excitement and was irritable when attempting to cut down or stop gambling. He also made repeated unsuccessful efforts to control, cut back or stop gambling. He was lying in order to maintain the addiction.

Gambling disorder is an illness that has a major impact on the individual and the people around them. When the illness is of moderate intensity, it is beginning to take over the person's life. In our next case study, Claire is engaging in behaviours that she would previously have thought unthinkable – she is lying to her husband and is secretly attending an amusement arcade. She also feels the urge to gamble and is unable to stop thinking about it.

CASE STUDY

Gambling disorder of moderate intensity

Claire is a thirty-year-old mother of two children, aged four and five. Her husband, Tom, is very busy with his new IT business. Claire and Tom have a number of stressful factors in their lives, not least the fact that Claire's mother has recently been diagnosed with Alzheimer's disease. In addition to looking after the children, Claire works full time in a local post office.

The demands on Claire are relentless. Money is also a worry for the couple. Tom lost his job during the recession and, to make matters worse, they bought a house just before the crash and have onerous mortgage repayments to keep up with. By the time the weekend comes around, Claire is exhausted. Of late, there has been little respite for Claire, as most weekends she cares for her mother with the aid of professional carers and other family members.

Claire's mother lives by the seaside and her house is quite close to an amusement arcade. While walking by, Claire noticed a commotion around one of the slot machines: someone had won what appeared to be a lot of money. Claire thought nothing of it on the day but the following week decided to give it a try. After a few spins Claire won the jackpot, €43. It wasn't the money that attracted Claire back to the arcade, rather the sense of release and relief. Claire was in another world in the arcade, relaxed, distracted and completely relieved of her usual stresses.

As each week passed, Claire spent more and more time in the arcade. She was also gambling more money to get the same feeling she got the day she won the jackpot. Claire started lying to Tom about where she was going. On a few occasions she told him that she was going to see her mother for the afternoon, when in fact she was at the arcade. Claire knew what she was doing was wrong, that she should not gamble as much as she did, but she felt strangely compelled to do so.

One particular week, she had decided that she would not attend the arcade but found that she couldn't stay away. She convinced herself that she had had a really difficult week and needed the break. Claire also realised that she was becoming unhealthily preoccupied with gambling. She could identify that she was unable to concentrate in work at times as she was craving being at the arcade.

Claire knew she needed to stop this secretive and potentially destructive behaviour. She spent two weeks trying very hard to stay away from the arcade. She then had an argument with the nursing staff caring for her mother, which really stressed her out. Before she knew it, she was back gambling again.

There were several other occasions where Claire attempted to stop but couldn't. Meanwhile, Tom had noticed a problem with their joint bank account, with many unexplained ATM withdrawals over the preceding months. The amount being withdrawn was increasing as time went on. Tom was convinced the debit card had been 'skimmed' and called the bank.

Later that evening, Tom told Claire about the issue and explained that the bank were looking into it. Tom tried to reassure Claire and told her not to worry, that it would all be sorted out. Claire broke down, revealing to Tom that she had spent thousands on slot machines at the arcade. Tom was shocked, not having any idea that Claire was engaging in this behaviour on a regular basis.

COMMENT

Claire's case demonstrates six DSM-5 criteria. She needed to gamble with increasing amounts of money to achieve the desired excitement. She often gambled when feeling distressed (stressed out, exhausted, worried about money). She lied to Tom to conceal the gambling and jeopardised her relationship because of gambling. She made repeated unsuccessful efforts to control, cut back or stop gambling (she knew she was gambling too much, attempted to stop but could not). She had frequent thoughts about gambling and planning the next gambling venture.

Severe gambling disorders are all-consuming and can wreak havoc not only on the individual but, as we see in this study, on families and loved ones.

CASE STUDY
Gambling disorder of severe intensity
David, a successful bar owner, is a well-respected figure in his community. He sits on several town committees and

has volunteered for a number of recent local community initiatives. David is happily married to Yvonne and they have three young children aged eight, five and three. David expanded his business in recent years with an emphasis on promoting sports within his bars. David's family have a well-established network of furniture stores. He helps out with this business, especially during busy times. His family are very grateful for this input.

David opened an online account with a major gambling provider. Prior to this, David had observed a lot of his patrons gambling in the pub and was curious about it. When he logged onto an online gambling site, he was pleased to see there was a free bet offer and he availed of this. He was also pleased to win on his first bet where he successfully predicted that Manchester United would beat Chelsea in an English premiership football game.

David subsequently won €3,000 on an accumulator bet. David had always felt his sports knowledge was good. Following these wins, he started to feel invincible. Although he was having the odd loss, in the main, he was doing really well. He was even starting to consider that gambling could be a new career. It made sense as he was aware of some local figures that apparently had made their fortunes through gambling. Gambling was such great fun to David and he now understood the excitement of the patrons gambling in his bar.

David started to increase his betting frequency and the amount of money he was betting with. He had also started to steal money from his family's furniture business. In David's eyes, this was not stealing – he was merely borrowing the money that he would inevitably be winning and would then put the money back without anyone noticing.

All went to plan when David won €15,000 on a Saturday afternoon. Instead of stopping and taking time out, David continued to bet. Gradually, however, things began to unravel. His time gambling now had increased substantially. He was lying about what he was doing. Yvonne knew something was wrong but couldn't work out what it was. Yvonne confronted David, with David denying there was any problem. For a few weeks, Yvonne was convinced David was having an affair. Again, she confronted him about this. More denials followed. David and Yvonne's relationship came under increasing strain as a result of David's covert gambling. David was now entirely preoccupied with gambling. He could think of nothing else. He knew he should stop and did try on a number of occasions, but to no avail. For a few days, when he was not gambling, he was restless and agitated. He went to Gamblers Anonymous on one occasion but felt it was of no use. Losses were really starting to mount now. David was feeling distressed but continued to gamble. He continued to take money from the furniture business. He was chasing losses now on a daily basis and gambling late into the night, telling Yvonne he was working on the bar's accounts.

On a Tuesday morning, David had dropped his two eldest children to school when there was a knock at the door. One of the managers of the furniture store wanted to speak with him. He broke the news to David that he had been seen on a number of occasions taking cash from the business safe. David was devastated by this news and, having made his excuses, got into his car and drove to a nearby lake.

All of David's plans to fix his gambling debt problems were up in smoke now. He arrived at the lake and suddenly felt an overwhelming sense of doom. Without thinking, David walked into the lake with the intention of drowning himself. Passers-by noticed what was happening and were able to persuade David to get out of the water. The emergency services were called and, following assessment by a Garda doctor, David was admitted to a secure unit of a psychiatric hospital. Yvonne was shocked when she received a call from the hospital.

COMMENT

David's case exhibits all DSM-5 criteria. He gambled with increasing amounts of money in order to achieve the desired degree of excitement. He was restless when attempting to cut down or stop gambling and made repeated unsuccessful efforts to control, cut back, or stop gambling. He was often preoccupied with gambling, being unable to think of anything else and often gambled when feeling distressed. He was chasing losses and gambling late into the night. He lied to conceal the extent of involvement with gambling. He jeopardised a significant relationship because of gambling. His marriage was under significant strain as a result of his covert gambling. Yvonne knew there was something wrong but could not work out what it was. He was relying on others to provide money to relieve desperate financial situations caused by gambling – in this case he was stealing from others.

SUMMARY

- Problem gambling is variously referred to as 'pathological gambling', 'disordered gambling', 'gambling addiction' and 'gambling disorder'. The most recent version of the American Psychiatric Association's classificatory system, DSM-5, refers to it as 'gambling disorder', which should replace other terms. Conclusive scientific evidence demonstrating the similarities of gambling disorder and other addictions led to a change in classification of gambling disorder from an impulse control disorder to the 'addictions' section. Gambling disorder is now considered to be an addiction like alcohol and drug addiction. This is an important classificatory change in terms of acknowledging the pain and suffering of those affected by the condition and will hopefully also reduce the stigma associated with the illness.

- Gambling disorder, like other addictions, presents on a spectrum ranging from mild to moderate to severe. To diagnose a mild form of the disorder, four to five criteria have to be present over a twelve-month period. To diagnose a moderate form of the disorder, six to seven criteria need to be present. To diagnose a severe form of the disorder, eight to nine criteria are required to be present.

Self-assessment tools are available to give an idea of the extent of difficulties one may have in relation to gambling. One such self-assessment tool is the Problem Gambling Severity Index, outlined on the following page.

Self-Assessment: Gambling Questionnaire

Thinking about the last twelve months …		
1. Have you bet more than you could really afford to lose?	Never Sometimes Most of the time Almost always	0 1 2 3
2. Still thinking about the last twelve months, have you needed to gamble with larger amounts of money in order to get the same feeling of excitement?	Never Sometimes Most of the time Almost always	0 1 2 3
3. When you gambled, did you return another day to try to win back the money you had lost?	Never Sometimes Most of the time Almost always	0 1 2 3
4. Have you borrowed money or sold anything to get money to gamble?	Never Sometimes Most of the time Almost always	0 1 2 3
5. Have you ever felt that you might have a problem with gambling?	Never Sometimes Most of the time Almost always	0 1 2 3
6. Has gambling caused you any health problems, including stress or anxiety?	Never Sometimes Most of the time Almost always	0 1 2 3

7. Have people criticised your betting or told you that you had a gambling problem, regardless of whether or not you thought it was true?	Never	0
	Sometimes	1
	Most of the time	2
	Almost always	3
8. Has your gambling caused any financial problems for you or your household?	Never	0
	Sometimes	1
	Most of the time	2
	Almost always	3
9. Have you felt guilty about the way you gamble or what happens when you gamble?	Never	0
	Sometimes	1
	Most of the time	2
	Almost always	3

TOTAL SCORE

Add up your scores from the individual questions. The higher the score, the greater the risk that your gambling is a problem.

Score of 0 = Non-problem gambling.

Score of 1 or 2 = Low level of problems with few or no identified negative consequences.

Score of 3 to 7 = Moderate level of problems leading to some negative consequences.

Score of 8 or more = Problem gambling with negative consequences and a possible loss of control.

Reference: J. Ferris and H. Wynne, *The Canadian Problem Gambling Index: Final Report*, submitted for the Canadian Centre on Substance Abuse, 2001.

CHAPTER THREE

MENTAL HEALTH AND GAMBLING DISORDER

Mental health problems are very common in gambling disorder, particularly in its more severe forms. This highlights the importance of nestling treatment services within or adjacent to psychiatric services. Our service at St John of God Hospital is situated within an acute psychiatric hospital, where many forms of expert acute psychiatric care are available.

Co-existing mental health and personality problems

The rates of nearly all psychiatric disorders are elevated in those who suffer from gambling disorder. Alcohol addiction is the most commonly co-occurring disorder. It is a common report that young men in particular tend to spend many hours alternating between the bookmakers and the pub. Higher rates of anxiety disorders have been found in those suffering from gambling disorder. This is hardly surprising as there is a great deal of worry involved – where to lay the next bet, how to get money to fund further gambling, how to pay back those that are owed money, how to keep hiding the behaviour. Being addicted to gambling is a stressful experience characterised by much fear and anxiety. Studies show lifetime rates of mood disorder – including depression as high as 70 per cent – in those suffering from gambling disorder. Again, being trapped in an addiction where even your closest allies don't know there's a problem will do little for your sense of well-being.

Personality disorder can be defined as a deviation of personality from the norm to the extent that it causes significant distress to the individual and those around them. Gambling disorder is frequently associated with antisocial personality disorder. I am often told by families that their loved one has become antisocial, reclusive, distant, uncaring, self-centred, even self-obsessed. Many of the features of gambling disorder, such as lying, manipulating and stealing, are antisocial by their nature. If there is a history of these antisocial features in the individual prior to the development of gambling disorder, clinicians will be asking whether the criteria for a diagnosis of antisocial personality disorder are met. This is not an easy diagnosis to make, especially when there are addiction issues present. Modern specialist addiction teams will have the input of clinical psychologists with expertise in the diagnosis of personality disorder. Psychologists will use a battery of tests to confirm the diagnosis. In many presentations, however, there is no prior history of antisocial behaviour at all. Indeed, the opposite may be the case: a history of a very caring, considerate and loving person who wouldn't dream of harming anyone. It is important to help families of those affected by gambling disorder understand that the features of gambling disorder illness are antisocial by nature and that with appropriate treatment, these features should decrease and eventually go away entirely. Much of the treatment in gambling disorder revolves around the promotion of pro-social behaviours, such as sharing, mutuality, humility, openness, compassion and forgiveness.

Other compulsive behaviours also co-occur at a higher rate for those with gambling disorder than the general population. Compulsive shopping and hypersexuality both occur at higher rates, most probably because they also involve abnormalities of the dopamine system. Parkinson's disease and restless leg syndrome are diseases essentially driven by low levels of dopamine. Drugs used to correct deficits in dopamine are known as dopamine agonists. It is commonplace for Parkinson's disease and restless leg syndrome to be treated with dopamine agonists.

In the early years of treating gambling addiction, our clinical team noticed increasing referrals from neurology departments of individuals suffering from Parkinson's disease. These individuals had developed gambling disorder as a result of taking dopamine agonist medication. Studies suggest that the prevalence of gambling disorder in Parkinson's patients can vary from 6 per cent in those not treated with a dopamine agonist to 17 per cent in those who are treated with a dopamine agonist. This finding adds significant weight to the concept that gambling disorder is a dopamine-driven brain disease.

Gambling disorder and suicide

Suicidal thoughts are common in gambling disorder, with rates in some studies reported to be as high as 90 per cent. Suicidal attempts are reported in up to 40 per cent of study participants. These figures suggest that suicide is a serious issue in the medical management of gambling disorder. This is borne out clinically where clinical services are vigilant regarding the potential of the person harming themselves. Clinical teams will ask specifically about mood problems, agitation, increasing despair, hopelessness, helplessness and anhedonia (an inability to feel pleasure in normally pleasurable activities). Sometimes it will appear very obvious to a clinical team that the patient is in trouble mentally. Other times it may not be so clear. Suicidal behaviour can be unpredictable and the very best of clinicians may fail to detect it due to the simple fact that the person wants to hide it. When a person feels they have nowhere to go, after chasing losses for months and accruing massive debts, suicidal thoughts can emerge.

Previous attempts of suicide or acts of self-harm increase the risk profile of the individual. Instilling hope at this stage is critical. It can be obviously very demoralising for individuals when they have to admit to months or years of lying and deceptive behaviour in addition to suffering major financial difficulties. Sometimes the patient requires close observation on a secure ward. The attitude that care-givers take at this point is all important as patients will, at times, despair and engage in catastrophic thinking. Those of us who have worked for many years on the front line treating gambling disorder will all agree: patients in the most desperate of situations can do very well and go on to happy, gambling-free lives. This is the aspect of working in addictions that is most appealing to me – to have the opportunity to work with patients who were so devastated by addiction but who find the motivation and determination to get well. The following case study of Kevin outlines the dramatic changes that occur from the initial admission to hospital with suicidal thoughts to long-term recovery years later.

CASE STUDY
Gambling disorder and suicidal thoughts

Kevin, a thirty-three-year-old married man, was referred by his general practitioner for acute psychiatric assessment. He had presented to his general practitioner earlier that day requesting help for gambling problems. He told his GP that his alcohol use and gambling had increased significantly over the last year following the loss of his job. Kevin also reported experiencing marital difficulties in the past few months. He hid his gambling problem from his wife but recently admitted to her that he was drinking too much. He had lost €6,000 in the previous few days and had failed to return home the night before, drinking in a hotel and gambling online. He denied any suicidal thoughts when he spoke to his GP.

Kevin was admitted to hospital later that day for treatment of gambling disorder. The admitting doctor felt Kevin was cooperative and polite but a little agitated. When the doctor asked about mood problems, Kevin stated that he felt depressed for at least two months. When the admitting doctor probed a little more, Kevin admitted to suicidal thoughts for the past week. He couldn't identify when or how they started but in the past few days was experiencing frequent thoughts of harming himself by walking into traffic.

He knew the thoughts were irrational and he had no intention of harming himself. Kevin was sure of this.

He told the doctor that he had no intention of inflicting any pain on anyone else through taking his own life. The admitting doctor was convinced by Kevin's indication that he would not harm himself. The admitting doctor also noted that Kevin had no history of self-harm. Kevin was restricted to the ward for twenty-four hours and gradually allowed to leave the ward for short periods. Gradually Kevin made a full recovery with intensive help. Four years later Kevin occasionally spoke about his experience of being admitted to hospital. He couldn't believe his mental state at the time. He was shocked at how he could have had thoughts like he did. Within Gamblers Anonymous, he frequently heard stories of how others had been similarly affected. This provided comfort and a sense that he was not 'weird' or 'abnormal'. He understood that gambling disorder is, at times, a severe illness that leads to suicidal thoughts.

COMMENT

Severe forms of gambling disorder may be complicated by suicidal thoughts. To complicate matters further, individuals who are suicidal can hide their thoughts and impulses. It is reasonable to ask individuals who present with severe symptoms of gambling disorder whether they are experiencing suicidal thoughts. As in Kevin's case, it is also helpful to reassure individuals experiencing suicidal thoughts in these circumstances that help is available and the thoughts will pass.

Effects of gambling disorder on the family

For every person affected by gambling disorder, it is estimated that seven other people are also affected, with family members bearing the brunt of the fallout. Relationships within the family are severely impacted by gambling disorder, with children especially affected. Treatment teams have a critical opportunity to engage and collaborate with patients and families at this juncture. It is very important that clinical teams instil a sense of hope during the early stages of engaging with patients and their families. This is because recovery is possible from all kinds of difficult circumstances. Hope is instilled by clinicians when they emphasise the fact that recovery is achievable. Otherwise, distress and despair can prevail, which does not help the patient or family.

Family members affected by gambling disorder present with varying levels of distress and trauma. Many family members – including parents, grandparents, siblings, spouses, uncles, aunts and children – present to our services for help (this help is outlined in chapters seven and eight). Gambling disorder can present at any age and forces many family members to react. In middle age, it can have a significant effect on elderly parents, who are suddenly thrust into caring for their adult children. Sometimes the problem presents whereby a husband's gambling is creating problems and we encounter the distress of the patient's partner.

I usually first encounter patients and their families within the setting of a first assessment appointment, where a GP has referred an individual suffering from gambling disorder to me.

Patients and families are usually unclear of what to do and how to proceed. The situation may be further complicated by the patient themselves lacking any insight into the extent of the problem. The patient may have presented in the context of a 'family intervention', whereby concerned family members have organised a meeting with the patient, confronting their addictive behaviours. These 'interventions' are often difficult, with family members venting a lot of pent-up emotion. Expletives can be exchanged and people can say things that they don't really mean or would choose not to say in other circumstances.

Patients can then present to this first appointment a little perplexed, upset and angry because, in their mind, the family have been 'conspiring' behind their back. Patients can also feel wounded when many family members 'unleash' their pain onto the patient.

Then there is the impact on children. As we have noted, the more severe forms of gambling disorder are characterised by intense loss-chasing. This leads to a severe form of preoccupation with gambling, which in turn leads to detachment from reality and normal family life. In this scenario, children will observe their parent becoming moody and distant. Sometimes the child will observe the parent being agitated, aggressive and sometimes even violent.

Most research to date has focused on the effect of gambling disorder on intimate partners and children. Where gambling disorder is present, relationships are characterised by poor communication, conflict, financial difficulties and sometimes even violence. Depending on the severity of the addiction, the children in these families report conflict, neglect, abuse and deprivation and are more likely to suffer from a range of mental health difficulties, such as conduct disorder, depression and antisocial behaviour. These children are also more likely to suffer from gambling disorder. International data also suggests that up to one third of presentations to various treatment services (face-to-face, helplines and web-based services) are family members affected by gambling disorder.

I have continually stressed that we regularly encounter patients and their families making amazing recoveries. These recoveries are often from what appear to be pretty daunting circumstances. In treatment facilities, I sometimes observe interactions between families and patients that are notable for their sense of hopelessness. This is understandable as some individuals will have attempted to cut down gambling on numerous occasions to no avail. We all want results, particularly family members that are affected by gambling disorder. It is easy to forget that all addictions, including gambling addiction, are relapsing and remitting conditions where multiple failures are sometimes a prerequisite to eventual success. One of the major positives of working in addiction services is observing patients who have struggled for years entering long-term recovery.

Questions to consider if you are worried about a family member's gambling

- Have you noticed your family member gambling more?

- Have you noticed your family member being more preoccupied with gambling?

- Are you aware of your loved one's current financial situation?

  [Do you have access to credit card and bank account statements, petty cash accounts and any other potential monetary transactions your loved one may be involved in? If not, a very good start is asking for access to these statements. Gambling disorder is usually plain to see on credit card and bank statements, where you will see an obvious excess of transactions to gambling companies. If your loved one is reluctant to share this information or you suspect they are hiding it, it may indicate a problem.]

- Have you had access to the mail recently?

  [One strategy used by those suffering from gambling

disorder is to intercept mail as it comes, then lying about its whereabouts or content. An example would be where the individual has accrued debt through disordered gambling and many demands from financial institutions for repayment of the debt are arriving in the mail. These letters are generally hidden or worse, not even opened. Insisting that bills are being looked after without any supporting evidence might be a subtle indication of a problem.]

- Have you noticed changes in phone, tablet, laptop or PC usage indicating a potential problem?

- Have you noticed a change in behaviour whereby your family member has become more isolated, moody, distant or aggressive?

  [Does your family member become defensive and/or aggressive when you enquire about excessive gambling? Does your family member appear physically or mentally unwell under the pressure of excessive gambling?]

- Has your family member been borrowing money from other family members or friends?

  [Sometimes it is worth asking the question directly if other evidence points towards a problem with excessive gambling.]

- Has your family member's interest in other activities declined in favour of gambling?

- Has your family member's sleep deteriorated? Are they pacing the floor at night worrying about money? Are they gambling at night when you are in bed?

- Have you noticed your family member becoming more unreliable? Have they committed to family events or meetings only to cancel at the last minute or not show up at all?

Tackling a potential gambling problem with a family member in a non-confrontational way

- Body language

    We communicate a great deal from our body language and facial expression rather than our words. If you are going to question your family member about the possibility of excessive gambling, sitting alongside your family member instead of directly opposite is a good start. Maintaining an empathic and compassionate disposition, even if you are feeling very angry, helps to keep the lines of communication open.

- Tone of voice

    As with body language, a great deal is communicated through our tone of voice, as well as by the content of our speech. Adopt as caring a tone as possible.

- Managing and containing angry emotions

    This helps prevent conversations developing into heated arguments. It is, of course, very tempting to unleash a host of emotions on a family member who has been lying, stealing and manipulating. Many family members transfer their anger onto the individual, usually to very little avail.

- **Language**

  Statements like 'you messed up', 'this is a problem of your own making', 'you're an addict' do not help to form collaboration. Try to avoid apportioning blame.

- **Compassion**

  Make it clear to your family member that you are motivated by compassion as opposed to anything else. Patients in denial may perceive any intervention as unnecessary meddling in their business.

- **Non-threatening approach**

  Avoid any exchanges that could be perceived as threats. Statements such as 'if you don't listen to me, you're out of the house' should be a last resort.

- **Benefits of change**

  Highlighting the benefits of addressing problem gambling is helpful; for example, 'Should you address this issue now, you will be much happier in the long run.'

- **Caring statements**

  Reminding the family member that you care for and support them is helpful; for example, 'We are family and I care about you – this is why I am trying to help you.'

SUMMARY

- Suffering from gambling disorder is in itself stressful, leading to a range of mental health problems including anxiety, depression and other addictions. This is why gambling disorder often requires the aid of psychiatric services.

- Antisocial behaviours are commonplace in gambling disorder. These behaviours are usually features of the illness that resolve with treatment of the illness. In some cases, these behaviours can be present before the onset of gambling disorder and persist after resolution of the illness, suggesting the presence of antisocial personality disorder.

- Gambling disorder is a serious medical illness, sometimes complicated by low mood, suicidal thoughts and suicidal behaviour. Suicide is a topic to be taken seriously in the treatment of gambling disorder as the rates of completed suicide are relatively high. The good news is that many people who experience suicidal thoughts in the course of gambling disorder recover and never experience suicidal thoughts again, going on to live happy, gambling-free lives.

- On average, seven people are directly impacted by one person's gambling disorder, usually family members.

RECOVERY

CHAPTER FOUR

TREATMENT AND STAGES OF CHANGE

For patients attending our treatment programme, a frequent question is 'How long can I expect to have cravings?' or 'How long do I have to continue to attend Gamblers Anonymous meetings'. The answer many professionals give to this question is 'lifelong', which in many senses is correct. It is also useful for those in recovery from gambling disorder to have a road map of how long each phase of recovery should take and what is involved. Each clinician will have their personal views on how long recovery should take. Some people make a decision to stop gambling and never gamble again, sometimes without accessing any professional help whatsoever. Others stop gambling and experience a mixed pattern of abstinence and relapse. Some have significant difficulties stopping gambling and seek professional help.

During months zero to six, energy is high and support from others is plentiful. New alliances are made within mutual support meetings and everything feels fresh. As the months go on, enthusiasm can wane. Similarly, those around the patient can tire of the effort involved in keeping up with recovery. Recovery can be exhausting for relatives. They can take on extra roles while the patient invests time in the various recovery inputs. In addition, checking on and worrying about the patient and their behaviours can be draining. Over time it is natural that spouses and relatives would enquire less about the patient. In some cases, spouses can resent all the care and attention the patient in recovery is getting from professionals. This is particularly the case when the patient is receiving treatment in the inpatient setting.

Key components of our treatment include providing therapeutic therapies, such as yoga, pilates and facilitated mindfulness sessions. When a spouse has to juggle looking after several children with work commitments, one can imagine that this would lead to some resentment. Spouses often say to me that they would like to be in the inpatient setting themselves to avail of the well-being therapies. The reality of addiction treatment is that the patient needs support, just like any other illness, even though it may be putting an additional burden on relatives.

During months six to twenty-four, or 'middle recovery', a lot of the hard work happens. Relatives are tired, the patient is tired and the prospect of further effort is not very appealing. Keeping the effort up during this stage is not easy and can even be punctuated by episodes of relapse. I witness plenty of situations where the patient does not relapse at all in recovery and this is fantastic. I also witness many other situations where the patient enters long-term recovery from twenty-four months onwards but has experienced a number of relapses between six and twenty-four months.

Although extremely difficult and upsetting for the patient and their family, this does not mean that they will not go on to long-term recovery. The key at this point is reassuring the patient. Relapse can serve as a timely reminder to remain vigilant at all times. It can also serve as a reminder of the awful consequences of gambling disorder – missed work, financial and relationship problems – all of which re-emerge during a relapse.

Nevertheless, time is required for the brain to transition from its addicted state back to that of normal function. The process is driven along by ongoing abstinence. During middle recovery, we also witness an increase in satisfaction in everyday activities. At first, engagement in everyday activities is dull, lifeless and lacking any real enjoyment. Over time and with continued abstinence, enjoyment in activities increases. These activities can be simple tasks, like grocery shopping or taking a child to school. As preoccupation with gambling lifts, a new renewed interest in these simple activities kicks in. Interest in previous hobbies also starts to increase slightly. We advise a return to hobbies in a gradual, phased way. For example, those previously interested in fishing would often say to me, 'I've no interest in that anymore, I just can't do it … no point.'

This type of statement reflects the void that is left after gambling hijacks the dopamine system. After the massive initial highs in gambling, everyday hobbies can seem drab and pointless. In this case, we would suggest starting with going to a tackle shop, speaking to the staff there. Another day, time can be spent attending one of the fishing spots, just observing or again speaking to some of the people there. Another day can be spent taking out all the gear, arranging and cleaning as necessary. Again, it is not unusual to be told that these tasks are a waste of time and there is no enjoyment coming from them. Finally, a trip can be organised to go fishing. Over many months, a sense of meaning returns to the activity, similar to the way it was prior to the development of gambling addiction.

Long-term recovery, from twenty-four months onwards, heralds the onset of a true gambling-free life. Patients are now genuinely engaged in non-gambling activities and deriving genuine pleasure from them. Preoccupation with gambling has reduced to very occasional bouts that are far less troubling than before. Some report complete resolution of any preoccupation. Research indicates that relationships generally repair and family structures, previously fractured as a result of gambling disorder, heal.

The transtheoretical or 'stages of change' model divides recovery into five stages. Although this model specifies exact time periods for each stage, the reality is that the timing of each stage will vary from person to person. No two recovery trajectories are the same. Relapse can occur during any stage, leading to an increase in the time involved to enter long-term recovery.

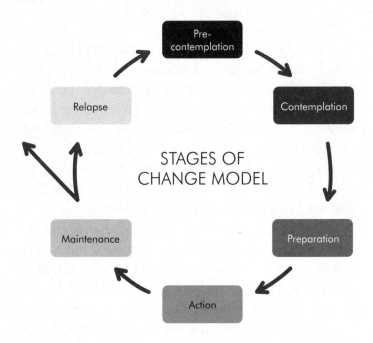

Transtheoretical model of recovery or stages of change model (Prochasha and DiClemente, 1983)

Pre-contemplative stage

In the pre-contemplative stage, the patient has not begun to consider change. It is often surprising for families when we describe a patient in clinical services being in a 'pre-contemplative stage'. This is perfectly normal, however, and, critically, is not the patient's fault. Gambling disorder, as an illness, specifically hijacks the motivational centres of the brain, preventing recovery. Impaired insight and a lack of motivation are key features of the illness, just as headache may be a feature of high blood pressure. Another concern of families is that the patient may be wasting time receiving treatment while in the pre-contemplative stage. This is not the case as time in the pre-contemplative stage is sometimes a natural prerequisite to progression onto the other stages of recovery. A huge benefit of the inpatient setting is that it can provide refuge from further gambling within a protected environment. Patients can remain safe and work on building motivation to move to the next stages of recovery.

Motivational interviewing (MI) is particularly helpful in nudging a patient's motivation along to the next stage of recovery. MI involves the use of 'decisional balance sheets' to demonstrate the pros and cons of continued gambling to the patient. The balance sheet, effectively a worksheet where different grids are completed, allows the patient to view the pros of abstinence in a logical and pictorial format. MI avoids the need for a therapist to be dogmatic or demand change because it emphasises collaboration and non-confrontation. Motivational interviewing provides a natural platform to help sufferers of gambling disorder to improve their drive to change. When choosing a counsellor to work with, it can be useful to enquire about the counsellor's use of and view of MI in their clinical practice.

Sample motivational interviewing balance sheet

Benefits of gambling	Benefits of not gambling
• Stress relief • Distraction • Convenient – click of a button • Fun	• Better relationships at home • More time for all activities • Better focus at work • Better physical and mental health • Better self-esteem • Less shame and guilt
Costs of gambling	Costs of not gambling
• Family income reduction • Unable to provide for children • Can't meet mortgage payments • Might lose home	• Less fun and contact with 'fun' friends • Less excitement around sporting events • Now I have no pastimes • Boredom

The following case study demonstrates that many patients enter treatment in the pre-contemplative stage in order to placate family members. Generally, insight into the nature of the problems are poor at this stage, with the patient themselves often convinced that they do not have a problem.

CASE STUDY
Pre-contemplative stage

Gerry runs a very successful carpet company. He has been gambling for over five years and the past year has seen his gambling increase significantly. He began drinking more in his local pub but also gambling in the betting shop a few doors down. In the past year, his wife, Patricia, has been very clear that Gerry's gambling has become problematic and insisted that he get treatment.

Gerry could see that Patricia was angry about his gambling and drinking so he agreed to take part in a rehab programme even though he felt that his wife was overreacting. On entering the treatment centre, he spoke openly with the admitting doctor. He told the doctor that he was only there for his family but was willing to do whatever needed to be done. The treatment team met with Gerry the following day. Gerry came across as cordial and collaborative but had little insight into the nature of his problems.

The team's social worker had contacted Patricia prior to the meeting and obtained a detailed collateral history. This history indicated very problematic gambling in recent times. Patricia outlined that Gerry had become increasingly consumed by gambling. He would not enter any conversation about it and repeated to Patricia that he did not have a problem. The couple's bank account suggested that there was a serious issue, however.

The treatment team addressed insight issues with Gerry. They explained the stages of change of addiction and also suggested that it was normal and acceptable for patients to be reticent at this stage of recovery. The team highlighted that it was not Gerry's fault that he was at this stage of recovery and that he would be supported through to other stages of recovery.

Gerry appreciated the input and felt that he was being supported rather than pressurised. He told his key worker after the meeting that if a different approach was taken – a more aggressive approach – he would have left the treatment centre and not come back.

COMMENT

There is no evidence that confrontational approaches to gambling disorder treatment are effective. The most effective approaches are supportive and patient-centred, assisting the individual to increase their motivation for change.

Contemplative stage

Following the pre-contemplative stage is the contemplative stage, whereby individuals are actively considering making changes to address their addiction. Clinical teams caring for patients with gambling disorder will be asking patients to reflect on the benefits and drawbacks of change. This is to draw out the reasons for change and to encourage the patient to move into the next stage, the preparation phase. It is very acceptable that a patient might have many reasons to continue gambling during the contemplative stage, such as distraction, stress relief, fun and being with 'fun' people (see 'Sample motivational interviewing balance sheet'). This is a normal feature of the gambling disorder illness. Gerry's case further outlines the shift in thinking from the pre-contemplative stage to the contemplative stage of addiction.

CASE STUDY

Contemplative stage

In the days following Gerry's initial meeting with his multidisciplinary team (which consisted of a consultant psychiatrist, nursing staff, psychologist, social worker and addiction counsellors), he had the opportunity to listen to many other patients' stories. Usually these conversations took place in the communal areas, the television area or outside in the gardens. He was given plenty of advice from other patients as to the merits of taking part in the inpatient treatment programme. He was advised that the programme was supportive, non-confrontational and compassionate in its approach and that it helped with well-being. The participants assured Gerry that he would gain considerably from both the group and individual therapy on offer. This was instrumental in Gerry deciding to continue on in hospital and take part in the addiction programme. This group of patients made it clear to Gerry that he would benefit from participating in the programme. They also emphasised that not long ago they were like him and unsure of how to proceed.

He made the decision to commence the inpatient treatment programme and spent the first few days listening to the facilitators and programme participants. Initially, Gerry thought that the programme had no relevance whatsoever to him. Gradually this thinking started to shift a little. Gerry was a little more open to the idea that his gambling may have been problematic. He also started to consider that his gambling had a negative effect on his family.

'Family day' for the programme was approaching. This entailed Patricia speaking to the team about the impact Gerry's illness had on her and the family. As Gerry expected, Patricia didn't hold back, giving a very real account of Gerry's problematic gambling. Whereas Gerry would have once discounted Patricia's account, he was now beginning to consider the impact of his gambling on her. He spoke to his key worker about a sense of guilt creeping into his thinking. His key worker suggested that this was indicative of him taking ownership of his behaviour in relation to his family.

COMMENT

During the contemplative stage of addiction recovery, contact with positive role models can be very helpful. This is often provided by mutual support groups such as Gamblers Anonymous. As in Gerry's case, it can also happen in the inpatient setting where there happens to be motivated and positive individuals. It is evident that Gerry's motivation increased and his thinking and behaviour started to change also. Professionals in addiction are trained to work with individuals at all stages of addiction recovery. Professionals are aware that many people present in the early stages of addiction recovery and are trained specifically to be encouraging and supportive rather than judgemental.

Preparation phase

Following on from the contemplative stage is the preparation phase, where the patient begins to plan active change and action is imminent. Many interactions with patients during this phase will be focusing on agreeing a clear plan of action. It is common during this phase for patients to continue to gamble while the planning is happening. It is also common for patients to start to reduce their gambling intensity during this period.

Mentally, the patient is shoring up their motivation to make active change. Patients are negotiating the plan, with their professional supports and most likely their family are part of the process. Arguments are plentiful during this stage. Families generally have a clear idea of what they want in the plan, whereas patients might have their own ideas. Friction can result and it is the role of the clinician to mediate in the process to broker a plan that everyone is happy with.

Should the patient share the plan with loved ones, it can increase investment and ownership. We are also told by patients that sharing the plan with loved ones increases pressure on themselves to succeed. During the preparation phase, we therefore encounter a degree of attrition where patients decide not to proceed with change. Sometimes staying in addiction can be the more attractive option as change can be too challenging or frightening. Occasionally fear turns to defensiveness and patients can actively resist change. Clinicians are trained to continue supporting the individual by remaining supportive and compassionate in the change process, knowing that many go through periods of resistance before eventually entering the action phase of recovery.

Action phase

The action phase is characterised by a cessation of gambling and it is the point at which a gambling-free life begins. Some aspects of the plan from the preparation phase are implemented and some are not. This is very normal during most recovery trajectories. Recovery from gambling disorder is not a 'game of perfect'. Not all aspects of the plan have to be implemented immediately. Achieving some elements of the plan is a success in itself.

Reiterating this success leads to further success. Patients become demoralised if the focus during the action phase is on what has not been achieved, rather than on what has. Cravings for gambling during the action phase may also be strong, so a great effort is required to maintain motivation.

The action phase can also involve the danger of relapse. This can be of huge concern to families affected by gambling disorder, who need to be assured that gambling addiction by its nature will be characterised by frequent relapse. The goal is, of course, to minimise the number of relapse episodes or to have no relapses at all. Nevertheless, it is important to highlight the fact that when a relapse happens, it does not mean that long-term recovery is unattainable.

CASE STUDY
Action phase
Tim was diagnosed with gambling disorder by a specialist and has been attending Gamblers Anonymous for several months. Tim has not enjoyed these meetings, speaking of

how it is 'just not clicking', and at times has been telling his partner that it is 'not for me'. At today's Gamblers Anonymous meeting, Tim was asked to speak. He did so, albeit a little reluctantly. He spoke of his struggles in recent months around staying motivated to stop gambling. He admitted to the group that on a few occasions he fell down, gambling for a day at a time. The GA participants were very clear with Tim that this was to be expected during recovery. One of the participants also gave a clear history of her difficulties with gambling. She spoke of her frequent relapses in the initial stages of recovery until she finally achieved long-term recovery.

It seemed to be a topic that resonated with the group because Tim noted that two other participants spoke about the same issue with a sense of conviction. With the support of Gamblers Anonymous and his specialist, Tim was able to gain much longer periods of abstinence over the following months and eventually started to feel a sense of determination during the action phase of recovery. Having initially felt like everything was a bit of a struggle, as time went on he felt a little more confident.

COMMENT

Gambling free days during the action phase of recovery allow the brain time to heal and gives an opportunity for the individual to adapt to a gambling free life. One should aim for total abstinence from gambling but if not immediately attainable, should aim to achieve as many gambling free days as possible.

Maintenance phase

During the maintenance phase, individuals start to realise the benefits of a gambling-free life. It represents the period from six months to several years. Once the period of several years is reached, one can be considered to be in long-term recovery. Pleasure is being derived from everyday activities. During the other stages of recovery, those in recovery may speak of not enjoying anything and crave a return to gambling. Gradually, interest in non-gambling activities increases.

The next case study demonstrates that during the maintenance phase of recovery, a sense of deriving pleasure from everyday activities increases. Family members will notice changes in the individual's behaviour in a positive way, with more engagement at home and fewer instances of moodiness.

CASE STUDY

Maintenance phase

Tim returned to his specialist to say that he had not gambled in two years. He spoke of an increased interest in hobbies he had previously neglected. He had returned to the GAA club where he had coached an underage team and was, for the first time in years, enjoying it. Preoccupation with gambling had reduced to the occasional thought, which Tim could deal with comfortably. Relationships at home had improved greatly also. When Tim was unwell, he was distant, detached and moody. Now he was genuinely engaged in home life and was determined not to return to a life of gambling. Occasionally he woke at night in a panic having dreamt about actively gambling but was able to return to sleep with ease, relieved that he was not gambling again.

COMMENT

Features of gambling disorder do not disappear entirely in the long term. It is perfectly normal to experience occasional mild preoccupation, cravings or dreams. These experiences may be unnerving for the individual but in the vast majority of cases they pass without a problem.

The biopsychosocial model

The 'biopsychosocial' model is used by clinicians to describe the different aspects of recovery. The biological category refers to any input that has the ability to improve functioning at a biological level. Examples in gambling disorder are getting professional help with sleep, seeing a dietician or nutritionist or taking medication (see 'Medication', Chapter Seven). Psychological inputs operate by improving the psychology of the individual to improve well-being and reduce gambling. Examples of psychological inputs in gambling disorder are cognitive behavioural therapy and motivational interviewing.

Gambling disorder social inputs are mainly lifestyle inputs. Social recovery strategies include exercise, lifestyle changes, controlling cash, reducing smartphone usage. Many of the inputs in recovery can span different categories. For example, Gamblers Anonymous is a 'social' input as it is mutual support without any professional help, but it most likely works at a psychological level also. All of these inputs are dealt with in more detail in the following sections and chapters.

Abstinence vs controlled gambling

One of the first decisions for the person in recovery is whether to give gambling up entirely or to cut down to a lower level. Most individuals in recovery feel abstinence is the best way to proceed as they have been affected by gambling in a negative way. In more severe forms of gambling disorder, it is obvious that the person should be encouraged to pursue a course of abstinence. However, this is often not clear to the individual because there are abnormal thinking patterns, which include a desire to continue gambling to put losses right.

Similarly, the prospect of a major change such as removing oneself from all gambling can induce anxiety. Abstinence presents many potential benefits and offers clarity to the individual and those around them. In abstinence, there is certainty that gambling will not be used as a form of recreation, stress relief, to alleviate boredom or to regulate emotions. There is no longer a need for lying, deception or manipulation of people and situations. There is also no need for borrowing or stealing money.

In less severe forms of gambling disorder, the person may be able to bring gambling back to a controlled level. It is the case that certain individuals may achieve this goal by being very vigilant and aware of their past problematic gambling. However, a major drawback with implementing a recovery strategy of controlled gambling is that in experimenting to see whether controlled gambling will work, the person may incur further losses and again suffer the consequences of gambling disorder.

SUMMARY

- Clinicians categorise recovery in stages as a means of informing patients and families of the different challenges along the road to long-term recovery. The staging is also helpful in that it can allow patients to realise that the intensity of the recovery process eases over time. Early recovery is from zero to six months and is characterised by high levels of energy, enthusiasm and support from family members. Middle recovery is from six months to two years and, because energy, enthusiasm and family support may wane, is liable to involve periods of relapse. Cravings may also increase as the enthusiasm of early recovery fades away. As recovery progresses, a greater sense of pleasure is derived from everyday activities and this pattern continues into long-term recovery (two years onwards) as long as abstinence is maintained. The transtheoretical model of addiction is one that breaks down the process into the pre-contemplative, contemplative, preparation, action and maintenance phases.

Dealing with debt as a result of gambling addiction

* Stop gambling

  Chasing gambling losses makes the situation worse. Committing to stopping gambling is the first and best step with regard to dealing with gambling debt.

* Tell a loved one

  Don't continue to hide the problem. By telling a family member or trusted friend, you are beginning the journey to recovery from gambling disorder.

* Protect against further gambling losses

  Transfer your salary to a family member's account and allow them to give you a non-negotiable amount everyday to cover essentials. In the event of relapse, damage will be limited as there will be no access to funds.

* Set up a repayment plan

  Where possible, devise manageable repayment plans with those who are owed money. As recovery progresses the debt visibly reduces, adding to a sense of achievement.

- **Seek the help of finance professionals**

  For example, the Money Advice and Budgeting Service (MABS, www.mabs.ie).

- **Mind your mental health**

  Although it may not seem so at the time, there is a solution to difficult debt scenarios. It is important to get the help of debt management professionals as soon as possible and avoid catastrophising.

CHAPTER FIVE
MUTUAL SUPPORT FOR GAMBLING DISORDER

Mutual support refers to self-help groups that are readily available in Ireland. Mutual support groups are the mainstay of non-professional help. The advantages of mutual support meetings are many: there is no requirement for referral from a doctor and a huge range of meetings are available nationwide. Meetings occur every day, three hundred and sixty-five days of the year. In the case of Gamblers Anonymous, the meetings are plentiful and do not require any pre-planning with regard to attendance. There is no obligation to contribute to the meeting, other than sitting in and being present.

I regularly advise patients who are reluctant to attend to do so firstly without feeling any pressure to contribute. Mutual support meeting participants are, on the whole, very welcoming and do not pressurise or judge newcomers. Being present in meetings is in itself therapeutic. Meetings are characterised by the promotion of prosocial activities. Mutuality, sharing of a common goal, the instilling of hope, caring, empathising and support are the polar opposite of addictive behaviours which are isolating, deceiving and manipulating.

Gamblers Anonymous suggests initially attending ninety meetings in ninety days. This suggestion has been present for decades, long before the scientific community started to investigate the powers behind mutual support movements. By repeating a certain activity, we practise it until it becomes familiar. By repeating a prosocial activity we are also undoing the antisocial behaviours that are so common in gambling disorder.

One of the key features of addiction is 'stereotypy' which is repeating the same behaviour over and over again in the same fashion. In gambling disorder, risk processing centres of the brain have been hijacked and the individual keeps repeating bad decisions. Whereas a controlled gambler might walk away following a losing streak, a problem gambler continues to gamble in the face of many adverse consequences. Repeatedly attending meetings gradually creates the environment the brain requires to heal.

If one was to continuously immerse oneself in a gambling environment, then eventually relapse would occur, as there is no opportunity for healing. Gamblers Anonymous has embodied this philosophy in its phrase 'people, places and things'. This refers to the concept that if you surround yourself with the right people, environment and life experiences, you will do well. Similarly, if you surround yourself with gamblers, attend betting shops or casinos and continue to use your smartphone, you are likely to run into trouble.

Some people have no difficulty attending Gamblers Anonymous meetings right from the outset. They have a natural affinity with the philosophy and are able to shrug off any negatives they may observe. Others have great difficulty attending meetings and offer numerous reasons to avoid them. In Ireland, the list usually begins with the complaint that meetings are too religious, too dogmatic, the participants too arrogant. Others tell me the meetings are depressing and when they leave they feel worse than when they went in. Another observation is that the other attendees are 'nothing like me' or 'much worse than me'. Some worry about the potential lack of anonymity. I'm often told that meetings are too repetitious, that the same people say the same thing week in week out. Others find meeting times don't suit their schedule – the list goes on and on. It's not that these aren't valid points. Meetings are far from perfect. Just like most therapeutic inputs in gambling disorder recovery, there are positives and negatives. Certain aspects of the approach will be appealing to some but will grate with others. I have encountered people who have great difficulty with meetings and have to drag themselves there day in, day out. This is often during the 'hard yards' of middle recovery (see Chapter Four) where motivation is not at its highest and the 'honeymoon' or 'pink cloud' of early recovery is long gone. However, we find that when an individual persists, they generally get something worthwhile from each meeting, and in our treatment centre we nearly always recommend attendance.

The twelve steps of Gamblers Anonymous (GA)

As a support network for gambling disorder, Gamblers Anonymous has a reach like no other, either in Ireland or internationally. Meetings take place almost everywhere in the country and there is no cost attached. No referrals from professionals are needed. The philosophy of GA is that gambling disorder is an illness that has to be managed through ongoing abstinence and cannot be cured. Gamblers Anonymous is a fellowship, meaning individuals are supposed to help each other and follow the twelve steps outlined here:

1. We admit we are powerless over gambling – that our lives have become unmanageable.

2. Believe that a power greater than ourselves could restore us to a normal way of thinking and living.

3. Make a decision to turn our will and our lives over to the care of this power of our own understanding.

4. Make a searching and fearless moral and financial inventory of ourselves.

5. Admit to ourselves and to another human being the exact nature of our wrongs.

6. Are entirely ready to have these defects of character removed.

7. Humbly ask God (of our understanding) to remove our shortcomings.

8. Make a list of all persons we have harmed and become willing to make amends to them all.

9. Make direct amends to such people wherever possible, except when to do so would injure them or others.

10. Continue to take a personal inventory and when we are wrong, promptly admit it.

11. Seek through prayer and meditation to improve our conscious contact with God as we understand him, praying only for knowledge of his will for us and the power to carry that out.

12. Having made an effort to practise these principles in all our affairs, we try to carry this message to other compulsive gamblers.

Staying in the process

Research suggests that the longer an individual stays in Gamblers Anonymous, the better they will do in recovery. Many of those suffering from gambling disorder attend one meeting of Gamblers Anonymous, deciding then that it's not for them. This is a shame as those who decide not to attend from the outset and those who drop out somewhere along the line do not do as well as those who continue over a sustained period. The benefits of staying with meetings are clear – a sense of mutuality, the regular instilling of hope and sharing of a common goal.

It is no exaggeration to say that GA can be life-saving. On occasion, I am told that attendance at GA has averted a plan of suicide where an individual was determined to harm themselves. For many, it can take up to six months of attending meetings before a sense of achievement sets in. Up to this point meetings can be dull and meaningless. The key is to persevere until a sense of achievement occurs.

The following case study outline's Jim's gradual acceptance of the merits of Gamblers Anonymous. The case highlights that, for many, it is not just a simple process of turning up for meetings.

CASE STUDY

Gamblers Anonymous

Jim always enjoyed gambling, but it was something he did very infrequently. Prior to meeting his wife, he and his siblings enjoyed betting on the Grand National and on the very occasional horse racing meeting. Unfortunately, he developed a severe problem with online gambling when he opened an online account. He lost all of his savings and deceived his wife, Mary, telling her lies for over a year. His problem gambling was eventually discovered when Mary noticed that her debit cards no longer worked. Further examination revealed more problems with various accounts. He eventually revealed his problem to Mary in a very difficult discussion.

Mary's uncle, Ted, had had a serious gambling problem about ten years previously. Mary and her extended family knew of the problem and asked Ted for help. Jim was not happy about the prospect of sharing any information with anyone, not least Ted, whom he didn't know well. Ted gave Mary his mobile number and gave instructions for Jim to call him if and when he would like to speak.

After much deliberation, Jim decided to give Ted a call to tell him that he had decided against attending Gamblers Anonymous meetings. During the phone call, Jim was impressed by Ted's attitude. He expected Ted to be pushy about attending meetings, which he was not. Ted told Jim that it was best to attend meetings when he felt up to it. Ted also reassured Jim that he could attend meetings and relax in the knowledge that he didn't necessarily need to contribute. Ted offered to meet Jim prior to a meeting and go to his first meeting with him. This approach worked very well, with Jim feeling encouraged after his first meeting. Jim continued to attend meetings, gradually becoming more convinced of the benefits of Gamblers Anonymous.

COMMENT

This case highlights the ambivalence that many experience around attending Gamblers Anonymous meetings. Jim, like many, was not initially amenable to sharing his personal information with strangers. However, over time and with some refection many make that initial step in attending a meeting. Following this, many are relieved to see that meetings and the people who attend them are welcoming and supportive. Over time, meetings can provide a huge support for those in recovery.

Participation in Gamblers Anonymous

As we have seen, the first step in participating in Gamblers Anonymous is simply to attend meetings. Merely attending meeting has its benefits. Surrounding oneself with recovery is preferable to not attending at all, and it is perfectly normal to attend meetings for a period of time with little participation. Contribution is not necessary in GA, but the more one participates the better. Addiction is characterised by repetitive, stereotyped isolated behaviour. To recover, the brain requires as much time as possible exposed to a positive environment. Meetings are characterised by positive behaviours – sharing, assisting, empathising and caring.

The chair will open the meeting and recount his or her own experiences with gambling addiction. This may last up to thirty minutes. Following this, the meeting is opened up to attendees for their input. Meeting attendees are aware that speaking comes naturally to some, but not to others. With ongoing attendance, the prospect of speaking becomes less of a concern for most people. Some meetings will have a specific theme, such as a 'Big Book' meeting where the chair will introduce particular topics from the Gamblers Anonymous reference textbook known as the 'Big Book'.

There is usually a natural progression from sitting in meetings, to contributing and eventually onto chairing meetings. Acting as secretary and organising refreshments are additional ways of making a valuable contribution. The more one contributes to meetings, the more opportunities there are to integrate with other fellowship members. It is not unusual to have unofficial meetings before or after the Gamblers Anonymous meetings, in a local café for instance. These get-togethers are a great opportunity for those in early recovery to glean tips and information from those in longer term recovery.

Serving as secretary or chairing a meeting are activities with a clear function in GA. Without these key functions, meetings would not happen. The effect on the individual from active participation at meetings are many – chairing meetings and acting as a secretary within Gamblers Anonymous require consideration, patience and humility. It is also remarkable how different one can feel after completing a very simple task, such as putting out refreshments for attendees. My advice to individuals in recovery is to take service and active participation at their own pace. If one doesn't feel up to graduating onto active service, leave it for a time that they do.

The next step after regular meeting attendance and active participation in meetings is to consider sponsorship. This entails having a 'sponsor' who will guide and be available to the Gamblers Anonymous member. It is possible to be sponsored after a few months of abstinence. People often ask how you 'get' a sponsor. This usually happens organically within a group setting where members of the fellowship become aware of an individual requesting sponsorship.

I advise individuals to let their regular group know that they are looking for sponsorship. This usually leads to a conversation between the individual and one of the more experienced members of the fellowship who might suggest an appropriate individual. The sponsor should be well into long-term recovery, usually of the same sex and motivated to guide and support the individual.

Gam-Anon

Gam-Anon has proven to be a strong support for those affected by addiction in Ireland. It is a fellowship of 'men and women who are husbands, wives, relatives or close friends who have been affected by a gambling problem'. The first response from family members can be: 'What's the relevance of that to me? I don't have the problem'. This is understandable as the first reaction from family is often surprise that they would need to attend meetings. Family members are key influencers in supporting and helping to bring about a recovery in their loved one. This is a primary reason for attending Gam-Anon: to educate oneself as much as possible on the approaches to take with a loved one. Gam-Anon currently reports on its Irish website:

> We learn at our Gam-Anon meetings that there is nothing we can do to stop our loved ones from gambling. If that is the sole purpose for attending meetings and you have come with a closed mind about yourself, then it is very likely that you will not return until you are desperate enough to want the help we can offer you. When this time

comes you will find many willing and friendly
members to help you with your problems.

gamblersanonymous.ie

This statement highlights the concept that family
members need to be in some way motivated to attend
and to be open to the process. I have observed some
families gain a huge amount of support from Gam-
Anon. As with Gamblers Anonymous, it is important
for family members to 'shop around' to find a meeting
that best suits them. No two meetings are the same,
with enormous variation in terms of atmosphere,
group dynamic and personalities within the group.
Some families tell me that they have had hugely
varying experiences within different meetings.

The following case study highlights the fact that
many people are apprehensive about taking part in
Gam-Anon. Some are even confused about the need for
a loved one to attend meetings. As the case outlines,
the benefits of attendance at Gam-Anon for loved ones
can be significant.

CASE STUDY
Gam-Anon
Pat and Bernie are attending an outpatient appointment
to see a consultant psychiatrist with their son, Justin. He
was referred by his GP to the psychiatrist for support with

gambling problems. While discussing supports for family members, Pat and Bernie were advised to attend Gam-Anon. Pat thought the specialist was making a mistake when suggesting himself and his wife attend meetings. Bernie had serious concerns about the confidentiality of the meetings and was reluctant to attend. They felt that it was not for them at this particular time.

Meanwhile, Justin experienced a difficult recovery from gambling disorder and relapsed a number of times. This was traumatic for Pat and Bernie, to the point where they felt they could not continue to support their son. Friends were advising them to 'cut Justin loose' and to get on with their own lives. It was at this stage that it was once again suggested that attending Gam-Anon might be helpful.

Pat and Bernie attended a meeting and were welcomed by the chairperson. They found the group to be very helpful and supportive. Bernie was no longer concerned about confidentiality as she felt things had reached a very serious point with Justin's problematic gambling. She felt any possible downsides with confidentiality were outweighed by the support she was receiving in the meetings.

Attending meetings became a regular part of Pat and Bernie's routine. They both felt a sense of support from the fellowship, particularly around managing their own emotions and were educated within the meetings around the concept of 'detachment'. They learned that their behaviours may have been exacerbating Justin's gambling problems. They learned that by offering food, accommodation and at times money they were enabling Justin. They became more aware of their interactions with Justin. They learned that sometimes they had no way of controlling his gambling and to protect themselves they had to 'detach'.

They were advised that they had to remove themselves as a support structure to Justin's ongoing gambling. The group spoke about co-dependence and how relatives can enable an addiction by continuing to support their loved one when they are in active addiction. Bernie struggled with this concept initially but over several meetings came to understand the importance of not reinforcing some of Justin's addictive behaviours. The couple also became familiar with the concept of 'detaching with love' whereby their decision to distance themselves from Justin was taken with their son's best interest at heart.

COMMENT

Co-dependence is a term used within the addiction field to refer to a dysfunctional relationship between an individual suffering from addiction and their loved one. If a relative provides accommodation, financial support or food for an addicted loved one they may be enabling ongoing addiction. The 'tough love' approach to this situation entails the relative detaching entirely from the individual to prevent 'enabling' further addiction. In doing so, the theory is that the individual is likely to hit 'rock bottom' sooner and ultimately emerge from addiction. For some relatives this makes sense and is something that they can follow through with. For others, it is unacceptable and cruel. Treatment teams will work with relative's preferences on dealing with ongoing relapse, as in the case of Justin.

Alternatives to Gamblers Anonymous

At present, there is no dedicated mutual support group alternative to Gamblers Anonymous in Ireland. LifeRing is a secular mutual support group available in Dublin (St John of God Hospital, St Patrick's Hospital) and some other cities which provides support for all addictions. Currently LifeRing holds meetings in Dingle, Mullingar, Navan and Tralee. The group also offers a women's only meeting. LifeRing describes its approach as follows:

> ... a new departure in self-help recovery. Thoroughly grounded in proven therapeutic approaches such as CBT and reality therapy, among others, LifeRing has also evolved out of the experiences of former addicts themselves. At the heart of LifeRing is the addicted person. We take charge of our own recovery in a mutually supportive and positive way. We accept that recovery is a matter of personal choice and responsibility. The group meeting is our main focus where we come together to share our experiences, to support and learn from each other on our individual journeys.

> lifering.ie

Many people suffering from gambling disorder in Ireland attend LifeRing for support and have found the meetings to be very beneficial. The format of meetings is to look at events of the past week and to share experiences with the other attendees. LifeRing differs from Gamblers Anonymous in a number of ways: it does not deploy the twelve steps process nor express faith in a 'Higher Power'. It does not look back at distant or past events in the way that Gamblers Anonymous can during the sharing process and does not offer a formal sponsorship process.

SUMMARY

Gamblers anonymous and LifeRing are mutual support groups for gambling disorder in Ireland. In the case of Gamblers Anonymous, meetings are held in many locations nationwide. The Gamblers Anonymous fellowship and LifeRing are excellent supports for those suffering from gambling disorder. In many cases individuals are reluctant to attend meetings as they are concerned about sharing personal information in groups. Others are concerned about what they believe to be the religious aspects of Gamblers Anonymous. If an individual is able to overcome these concerns and attend meetings, they increase their chances of entering long-term recovery. Loved ones supporting an individual affected by gambling disorder can attend

Gam-Anon meetings where they can receive support from other individuals who have been through the process of gambling disorder recovery.

CHAPTER SIX
SELF-HELP STRATEGIES

Controlling your environment

Controlling one's environment during recovery is a key strategy in getting well. A phrase from Gamblers Anonymous is 'if you stay long enough in a barber shop you are likely to get a haircut'. This refers to the idea that if the environment is triggering, then it is only a matter of time before relapse occurs. Recovery from gambling disorder ultimately involves distancing oneself from certain friends and acquaintances. The people around the person in recovery are critical to the success of the individual. If one wants to be sure that they are not surrounding themselves with problem gamblers, the only sure way to know is to avoid gamblers and gambling places entirely.

Managing loneliness and isolation is a key factor in ensuring the best possible environment for recovery. Problem gambling is ultimately an isolating behaviour. Whereas controlled gambling may have a social aspect to it, problem gambling usually entails long hours spent alone, either in a bookmaker or on a phone. Gambling disorder can often develop as a way of regulating emotions and providing comfort and escape from unpleasant life situations.

When an individual is under stress and does not utilise positive adaptive responses such as meeting friends, exercise and hobbies, problem gambling can provide an outlet. In stopping gambling, a void is created whereby the individual can feel like a major and important part of their life has been removed. This can be likened to a grief reaction as the attraction and investment in the behaviour is so substantial. Being unable to watch live sport, unable to gamble online or attend a casino can be manageable in the first month of recovery.

Following this however, things can get a little more challenging. Managing loneliness and isolation by engaging in positive activities, meeting friends and family, attending mutual support meetings and engaging in voluntary work in the community are examples of ways one can reduce the potential of loneliness and isolation in recovery. Recognising that emotions of loneliness and isolation will not last is also important. These emotions are most prominent during middle recovery (months six to twenty-four) but gradually fade over time with continued abstinence.

Restricting viewing of live sport

Our own research data from the National Online Gambling Survey, published in 2017, indicates that sports betting is one of the most common forms of gambling in Ireland. If problem gambling is based on sports betting, it is very important to devise a strategy that specifically targets it. When negotiating care plans with patients in treatment there are various approaches that can be used based on the preference of the individual. For some, all sport has to be avoided.

This is usually the case in severe gambling disorder whereby any exposure to gambling is problematic. This may mean not attending coveted sports events that the patient would dearly like to attend. Such is the sacrifice involved in becoming gambling free. In milder forms of gambling disorder, not watching live sports can be a less severe but successful strategy. Games are recorded and watched at a later date where there is no opportunity to gamble in real time. A frequent question relates to how long these restrictions should be in place. This really depends on the progress one is making. All cases differ, particularly the level of relapse and the length of the periods of abstinence achieved. If a patient is doing well, why would you change anything, including restricting access to either watching or attending sport? Eventually (at least two years) the patient can negotiate a return to watching or attending sporting events within a gambling-free life. In milder forms of gambling disorder, it is also the case that patients will report difficulties with one sport, for instance horse racing only. These patients have never gambled on other sports and have no difficulty watching these sports.

The next case study outlines the difficulties that exist in managing exposure to sporting events in recovery. Ideally, all exposure to every sport should be eliminated, but this is very difficult to achieve. Richard's case outlines that the approach to live sports often evolves with ongoing negotiation with the person in recovery. Re-exposure to sports can be completed in a graded fashion, from no access, to access to pre-recorded events, to access to live sports.

CASE STUDY
Viewing live sports

Richard was discharged from the inpatient setting four weeks after he successfully completed an inpatient treatment programme for gambling disorder. As part of Richard's discharge plan, it was agreed that he would avoid watching all sports, live or otherwise, and would not attend any sporting events.

In the past few weeks, Richard has been doing well with no reported gambling. He attended his meeting with his specialist, reporting that he was unhappy with the fact that he could not watch any sports whatsoever. Richard was strongly of the view that because his problem gambling was entirely based on horse and dog racing, it was unreasonable to prevent him viewing other sports. He argued that there was no risk involved with him watching these sports live. Richard's specialist spoke about the potential for substituting the dog and horse gambling with other sports gambling. His specialist explained that it was common for substitution to occur and that Richard should be mindful of this. It was noted in the meeting by his family that Richard had agreed not to watch any sport going forward.

After much discussion, it was agreed that Richard would continue to avoid watching any sport for the next four months, until six months of abstinence. Following this, it was agreed that Richard could watch pre-recorded sports events on television but not attend any live sporting events. It was also agreed that Richard would avoid dog and horse racing entirely.

COMMENT

Disagreements between the individual in recovery and their loved ones are common in recovery. So too are disagreements between clinicians and the individual in recovery. It is unreasonable to expect that all interactions between the individual and their support team are going to be entirely friction free. Clinical teams experience friction within the therapeutic relationship on a daily basis. The vast majority of these disagreements are resolved through understating and supporting the person in recovery and agreeing on an outcome that is acceptable to all.

Removing access to online gambling sites

Nowadays, the vast majority of people own a smartphone, enabling instant online access to a full suite of gambling products. Encouraging patients to remove the smartphone from their lives, or at the very least restrict access, has become a key feature of our care plans. Reducing smartphone access is also a central theme during the action phase of recovery. For those who have gambled online, the smartphone is the predominant portal through which destructive gambling occurs. Patients also report gambling on PCs and laptops but to a much lesser degree. For some, changing from a smartphone to a non-internet connected device is a step too far, unacceptable on many levels. Some patients require a smartphone for work, particularly to access emails and changing to a non-smartphone is not an option. Younger patients may rely heavily on social media platforms to interact with friends. So, naturally this topic is going to raise emotions. Some patients will continue to use a smartphone with access to email and the internet but will block access to any gambling sites with the relevant software (e.g. Gamblock).

Self-exclusion from gambling sites is the most commonly offered consumer protection in Ireland at present. Self-exclusion should have an option for life and should be enforced stringently by the gambling operator. This is often not the case. A few simple steps from the patient should be enough to remove all access to online gambling. It is not unusual, however, for the individual to have to ring a call centre to have an account shut down, rather than being simply able to do it online.

Our own research shows that many more consumer protections exist which are not widely available in Ireland. For instance, loss limits and betting limits are not readily available to many gamblers. Similarly, it would be very helpful if deposit limits were mandatory on Irish websites. To date, any available consumer protections for Irish gamblers are voluntary but as gambling disorder takes hold in an individual and compulsion increases, it is unlikely that the individual will set such limits voluntarily.

Managing acute and post-acute withdrawal symptoms

The effects of gambling withdrawal, like the effects of substance withdrawal, are time limited. Immediate effects of substance withdrawal last days to weeks. Gambling disorder is no different where the individual can feel physically ill and have strong cravings for gambling. Following the initial phase of withdrawal is the 'post-acute withdrawal syndrome' phase where withdrawal symptoms remain present but to a lesser degree. Mood and motivation are decreased, energy levels are not optimal and the person can generally feel out of sorts. Cravings to gamble continue but usually at a reduced level. These symptoms eventually disappear, as do loneliness and isolation. The key is knowing that both acute and post-acute withdrawal symptoms are limited.

It is impossible to tell in any given individual how long these symptoms will last, but all recoveries share a gradual reduction in these symptoms over time. The problem, on occasion, is that these post-acute withdrawal symptoms can get on top of the individual. A frequent cause of this is that the person has no sense of a road map of their recovery, feeling that they will be preoccupied and craving indefinitely. This, unfortunately, can lead to depression and anxiety. Responding to post-acute withdrawal symptoms in a positive way is critical. Examples, outlined in this chapter, are attendance at mutual support meetings, mindfulness, exercise, self-care, development of new hobbies, removing access to online gambling sites, managing funds, development of new hobbies, sacrifice, rewarding oneself when appropriate, substituting addictive behaviour with less damaging behaviours when appropriate and dealing with setbacks.

Mindfulness, exercise and self-care

The evidence for the efficacy of mindfulness in aiding mood and anxiety has strengthened in recent times. For years, we were aware that mindfulness was an effective stress reliever at a clinical level. Recovery is aided by practising staying in the present moment and not projecting into the future. A lot of anxiety is based on the inability to stay present in the moment, instead catastrophising on possible future events. Addiction is also characterised by a tendency to control events and project in a worrying fashion towards the future. Mindfulness teaches us to practise leaving things as they are and reduces our tendency to ruminate on things we cannot control.

The serenity prayer in Gamblers Anonymous reflects concepts from mindfulness, asking for strength to know the things that one can control and those that one cannot. Mindfulness takes time and plenty of practise. Some get stress relief from the meditations immediately, whereas others take longer to benefit from such practices. Some give up after a while, citing no benefit or having little time to engage in the practices.

As with many recovery inputs, time and perseverance are required. For most, at the very least, mindfulness offers an opportunity to get away from gambling thoughts and allows the body to unwind.

Exercise has demonstrated beneficial effects in stress, mood improvement and drug addiction. Significant benefits have been described with as little as ten minutes of exercise a day contributing to a reduction in mortality of 13 per cent. An analysis of thirty-nine studies of exercise in the treatment of depression revealed that exercise has an effect similar to psychotherapy. Studies of alcohol addiction report significant reductions in alcohol intake and binge drinking. A study of exercise and gambling disorder, albeit in a small sample from São Paulo, Brazil, indicated that moderate intensity exercise may be helpful where there are other conditions occurring with gambling disorder such as stress, anxiety or depression.

Restoring sleep and establishing healthy bio-rhythms helps elevate a sense of well-being after periods of excessive gambling. This is because gambling disorder is characterised by a lack of self-care and poor sleep patterns which can give rise to additional health problems. As a good deal of online gambling can occur at night, sleep can be reduced. Altered sleep patterns can persist long after the person has stopped gambling. In many cases, all that is needed is to prioritise healthy sleep patterns and simply allow enough time for adequate sleep (six to eight hours generally being accepted as the norm). If sleep does not correct itself, then there is the possibility of being prescribed short-term medication or seeing a psychologist for cognitive behavioural therapy. Eating habits are also affected by gambling disorder. I have encountered patients who had to rely on handouts or go without meals as they had run out of money. Reestablishing a healthy eating pattern also helps to elevate a sense of well-being.

Managing funds

For the first two years of recovery, it is worth thinking carefully about access to cash, credit cards and any type of banking facility. Although the individual may not be experiencing cravings and has no intention of gambling, if there is ready access to funds, the risk of gambling increases. Gamblers Anonymous has a saying about the 'cunning, powerful and baffling' nature of gambling disorder. When you speak to individuals after relapse, there is often a sense of confusion as to how the event happened. Relapse can be swift as the rational thinking of the individual evaporates and craving escalates. A simple but effective measure is to prevent the potential for gambling by not having access to cash or credit. For most, it is impossible to function without any access to cash whatsoever. A practical approach is to allocate a set sum, say €15 a day, to cover travel, lunch and snacks. This sum will vary depending on the individual's needs and circumstances. This money can of course be gambled where the individual is determined to do so. Damage is limited, however, as the individual could gamble with a lot more money but does not have access to it.

This is an example of the principle of harm minimisation. This is not a popular suggestion to those in recovery, because it is perceived as authoritarian by the patient and is often resisted. Nevertheless, giving over control of the finances to the loved one, spouse, trustworthy friend or relative is a very good idea in recovery. The more money that accumulates the better. As debts are repaid, it serves as a sense of achievement and fuels further motivation to keep transferring money to a relative or close friend. The process need not last forever. After at least two years (although this varies from case to case), a discussion can occur around increasing the individual's access to funds. It should be noted that the process is not a panacea.

In this case study we observe the very real difficulties encountered by individuals in recovery when it comes to managing finances in gambling disorder. As is often the case, handing over one's monthly finances is not an enticing prospect.

CASE STUDY
Managing funds

Shane presented for treatment after being referred by his GP. He gambled in a harmful way for over a year, meeting the criteria for moderate gambling disorder. Shane and his partner, Marie, have attended their first outpatient appointment with their specialist. A plan was formulated which included a recommendation that Marie take full control of Shane's finances. Shane said very little about this at the first appointment.

On the way home from the appointment Shane was very angry and resentful. He told Marie, in no uncertain terms, that he would not be handing over any money. He said it was an outrageous suggestion and questioned whether the doctor knew what she was talking about. Shane went to bed that night in foul humour.

Marie was stressed by Shane's reaction. She was also resentful, as in her mind she had been put through enough without having to endure this behaviour. Shane relapsed three weeks later, reattending casinos after meeting his friends for drinks. At the next meeting with their specialist, Marie raised the fact that Shane had not been handing over funds to her. A discussion ensued and, following this, Shane agreed to transfer all of his earnings to an account that only Marie had access to.

Four years later, recovered from gambling disorder, Shane speaks about how this intervention was key in his recovery. He was able to see money building up from his regular pay cheques. He was also able to start paying off gambling debts that had been at the back of his mind for a long time. These changes helped to build up Shane's motivation gently until he became more convinced of the benefits of stopping gambling.

COMMENT

Conflict is commonplace in gambling disorder recovery. It is a difficult time for all, so it is no surprise that things flare up every now and again. Shane, although initially annoyed and defensive, was able to move to a situation where he agreed to share management of his finances with his partner. He demonstrated flexibility and openness in the recovery process which are positive prognostic factors.

Development of new hobbies

Gambling disorder strips an individual of their interests over time. This reflects a feature of gambling addiction referred to as 'primacy' or 'salience'. As addiction takes hold, focus on gambling intensifies until the individual is preoccupied with nothing other than gambling. In more severe forms of gambling disorder, the preoccupation is all-consuming, leaving no room for any other interests, including work and family. Development of new hobbies in recovery is not an easy task at first, with patients sometimes reporting that they have very little interest in anything (see Chapter Four).

Gambling disorder is an illness that has profound effects on the motivational centres of the brain. The patient has to be encouraged to become motivated in new activities. A good place to start is activities the patient engaged in prior to the development of gambling disorder. Some patients tell me that they had no interests in the past except gambling. This is a little more challenging in that the patient has to focus on developing new activities and interests. The list of potential interests is, of course, endless and really depends on the individual. The benefits, interests and hobbies present in recovery are important on many levels. Some offer physical exercise which helps with stress reduction and mood (see 'Mindfulness, exercise and self-care' in this chapter). Hobbies also offer new environments for the individual in recovery. Prior to recovery, many hours each day are spent gambling and many more are spent preparing and organising the funds to gamble. The more the individual immerses his or herself in a new non-gambling environment the better. The more the patient's recovery is focused on the dangers of 'gambling people', 'gambling places' (bookmakers, casinos, race meetings, card games) and 'gambling things' (smartphone, excess cash) the better for them in the long run.

Sacrifice

Some individuals presenting to our treatment centre recover from gambling disorder with little effort and sacrifice; however, these fortunate individuals are generally in the minority. Gambling disorder recovery involves parting with a once loved behaviour. As the months go by in recovery, 'euphoric recall' often arises. This is a form of disordered thinking whereby the individual reminisces on the good times of gambling, forgetting the misery that followed afterwards. When euphoric recall is protracted, it can lead to relapse.

Addiction as an illness is characterised by frequent relapse as the individual is convinced, through faulty thinking, that returning to gambling will be pleasurable. Similarly, gambling disorder is complicated by cravings to gamble and a wish to chase previous losses. Chasing behaviour can also re-emerge at any stage in a recovery. This is why vigilance is so important with regard to 'people, places and things'. A key question is to what extent the patient needs to implement a strategy to avoid triggering 'people, places and things.'

The first issue is people. One ideally will avoid contact with gambling friends. People are sometimes not entirely honest with themselves about how much their friends influence their gambling behaviours. The issue can be particularly difficult in young individuals where gambling is prevalent within the peer group. Ideally, the young person will avoid all gambling peers in an effort to avoid relapse. Sometimes this is not feasible and isolating a young person from the peer group may cause more harm than good. The more severe the gambling disorder however, the stronger the argument to avoid the gambling peer group. This then may indeed mean dropping a certain peer group with a view to developing new friends that do not gamble.

The issue of places can be straightforward. Avoid betting shops, race meetings, casinos and other places that are triggering. Sporting events present more of a challenge in relation to how to proceed (see 'Restricting viewing of live sport' in this chapter). Also, I have treated patients who work in sports bars where there is a good deal of gambling within the bar. The patient may not be in a financial position to leave this employment or may even own the bar. This reflects the fact that not all areas of recovery are controllable at a given time.

One has to control as many of the variables within 'people, places and things' as possible, devising a care plan with as many positive inputs as can be achieved in the circumstances. This patient has to get on with their recovery while in close proximity to gambling twelve hours a day, six days a week. This is sometimes the reality and I have encountered excellent recoveries in these situations. Usually, the person will invest heavily in activities and recovery strategies that they have control over, such as the ability to attend meetings, exercise, develop new hobbies, see a counsellor, avoid smartphone usage for a specified period and hand over all cash for at least two years. We have already considered things to avoid when discussing smartphones and managing cash in previous sections.

Rewarding yourself

Many people in recovery forget to take a breath and reflect on the progress they have made. Several months can pass in gambling disorder recovery where the person is driving themselves as hard as possible. Not often enough does the individual stop and reward themselves for gambling-free days. It is possible to help that process along by rewarding oneself after a period of abstinence. Sometimes there is a slight over-focus in recovery on paying back debts and lost money through gambling. Reinforcement of positive progress leads to more progress.

Substitution

After cessation of gambling, many report an increase in appetite or a craving for sweet food. This is a regular point of discussion in outpatient clinics.

Chocolate is often reported as the 'new addiction' but this craving simply represents a temporary substitute for the gambling addiction. Weight gain is also not uncommon as increased calories are consumed. It is true that changes in diet that include junk food and chocolate are not ideal in the short term, but a resumption of gambling is frankly a much worse proposition. Temporary behaviours such as sugar craving and increased calorie intake largely subside over time and should not be worried about while abstinence from gambling is maintained.

Dealing with setbacks

Setbacks are very common and a natural part of recovery. In recovery from gambling disorder, relapse is an obvious setback, but there can also be many other things in life that occur during the course of recovery. A member of the family can become ill, a partner can fail an exam, a road traffic accident or a burglary can happen. Positive events in life can also be stressful – a job promotion, weddings, family events and celebrations. While recovery is underway, life continues with all its ups and downs. Where gambling may have been used to regulate emotions, now life's stresses need to be navigated without it. Being involved in one-to-one addiction counselling (see Chapter Seven) or attendance at mutual support meetings can be a great help in dealing with stresses as they arise. Simply knowing that recovery is at times not going to be straightforward is also helpful; reminding oneself that staying gambling free during these periods is most important.

Dealing with despair

Common questions from both patients and families are: Why me? Why us? There may not be a family history of addiction or mental health disorders. This may lead families to question why the problem arose in their family. Similarly, the patient may have been very highly functioning prior to the emergence of gambling difficulties. The best current evidence suggests that the answer lies both in nature and nurture, meaning that addiction problems run in families but can also occur sporadically. Environmental exposure to gambling, particularly during adolescence, is an important non-genetic influence in problem gambling. When family members have no previous experience of dealing with addiction it can be very shocking to discover a family member is suffering from the illness. The period of initial engagement with services can be challenging and tiring. Clinicians appreciate that patients and families do not want to be affected by gambling disorder, this is obvious. Clinicians are also aware that families despair when relapse occurs in addiction.

A family's hopes and fears are wrapped up in the patient remaining well. When relapse occurs we understand that it is devastating for all concerned. Treatment teams are trained to deal with these difficult situations. Families are often also concerned that they have caused the problem. In the vast majority of cases, families play little or no role in the genesis of problem gambling in the individual. Treatment teams will be keen to reassure family members that they have not caused the problem, that it is not their fault and that they should focus on their own self-care. This includes advice on attending local Gam-Anon meetings, attendance at one-to-one counselling, continuing with a regular routine and avoiding further conflict.

This case study captures the intense despair that relatives experience when their loved one is struggling with gambling disorder. Over time, relatives and loved ones find ways of coping with the pain of gambling disorder.

CASE STUDY
Dealing with despair

Frank and Mary are happily married with three grown up sons, Alan, Brian and Peter. Alan and Brian are both successful accountants. Peter, always considered to be the most intelligent member of the family, studied maths at university. He is very popular with his peer group and is an active member of many of the sports and arts clubs in university.

Unfortunately, Peter developed a severe gambling problem with online casino products. He amassed a debt of €10,000 while in his first year of college. His parents made the decision to pay these debts for Peter by remortgaging their home. Peter insisted to his parents that there would be no further difficulties with gambling. He attended GA and also attended a local counsellor who had an interest in problem gambling. Frank and Mary were convinced that Peter had put his problems behind him. Peter relapsed again, this time with more complications. While working part-time in a pub, Peter was caught stealing from the cash register.

Peter revealed that on this occasion he had amassed a debt of €50,000. Frank and Mary were speechless. They felt completely numb and powerless. Anger was always present now as Peter had lied consistently to hide his ongoing gambling. Peter was admitted to the inpatient setting of a psychiatric hospital. As part of Peter's treatment, Frank and Mary were seen by the consultant psychiatrist and the social worker. Both meetings revealed that the couple was very distressed and traumatised by recent events. The clinical team explained to Frank and Mary that it was not their fault that Peter had developed the illness of gambling disorder. Both parents had displayed helplessness but also a lot of guilt. Engagement with a one-to-one counsellor was recommended for the couple. Attendance at the mutual support group Gam-Anon was also recommended.

Through the various supports put in place for Frank and Mary, they gradually felt the sense of despair lifting. Although far from easy, they were able to regulate their own emotions better now with the professional help that they were receiving. Ten years on, Peter has not gambled in years. Frank and Mary continue to attend Gam-Anon. They provide support and wisdom to couples who attend these meetings for assistance with a loved one suffering from gambling disorder.

COMMENT

The case of Frank and Mary highlights the levels of distress family members can encounter when dealing with gambling disorder. As we have already emphasised, like all addictions, gambling disorder presents in a relapsing and remitting fashion. Relapse can be very challenging for family members, especially when large sums of money are lost. This case study outlines the desperation that can occur and the importance of support structures that can play a key role in helping loved ones move on from despair.

SUMMARY

Many people make full recoveries from gambling disorder without the help of professionals. There are many ways a person can help themselves to recover from gambling disorder. Practical measures such as handing over funds to a trusted family member or close friend reduces the risk of further gambling. In the case of problem online gambling, choosing not to use a smartphone reduces the risk of further gambling. Other practical measures include self-exclusion from gambling sites and avoiding watching live sport. A successful recovery from gambling disorder is likely to involve sacrifice, but can be made less painful by the occasional rewarding of oneself and the development of new interests and hobbies.

CHAPTER SEVEN
SPECIALIST HELP IN THE OUTPATIENT SETTING

The first step in receiving specialist treatment is usually attending an outpatient appointment. Referrals to addiction clinics are by a general practitioner (GP) concerned about the gambling behaviours of the individual. In order for a GP to make a referral, there must have been some concern on the part of the individual or the people around the individual about problem gambling. Patients may have had little in the way of support prior to attending. There is usually a considerable amount of anxiety for the individual and family attending this appointment. The patient may have very little insight into the extent of the problem at this stage. They may feel they have a relatively minor difficulty, whereas the evidence and view of the family is that there is a much bigger problem. They may also have concerns about stigma or embarrassment.

While some presenting for treatment have little or no insight, others have truly hit rock bottom. These people have surrendered to the fact that they have been powerless in the face of the addiction. They have come to a point in their lives where they can admit to themselves and to the people around them that they have a problem. They have accepted that they cannot gamble in a controlled fashion and are aware that they need to actively avoid gambling triggers. They may have suffered a humiliating event or seen the effect of their gambling on their children. Others may be fed up with the way gambling has affected their most cherished relationships, deciding enough is enough. Sometimes money drives the individual to instigate change. They cannot tolerate any more losses.

Prior to 'hitting rock bottom', it is common for the individual to question if they can gamble in a controlled fashion. Sometimes the person has attempted controlled gambling on several occasions until eventually surrendering to the reality that abstinence is the only viable option. One of the central features of a dependence state is 'rapid reinstatement after abstinence'. This refers to the concept that once you gamble at a particular level in a problematic way, it is unlikely that you can lower your gambling to a more benign level. Periods of abstinence are usually followed by resumption of gambling at the same level as before. This is often experienced by the individual prior to finally deciding to move on with total abstinence.

Outpatient treatment

Participating in an inpatient rehab programme is not an option for many individuals. There may be no availability in the locality or it may be too expensive. Some are fortunate to have insurance cover, others are not. The time involved in completing an inpatient programme may be a problem for some and arranging childcare can also pose a difficulty. Outpatient treatment may be the only viable treatment option for many individuals. There is little evidence to suggest that outpatient treatment is inferior to inpatient treatment in terms of efficacy. Following a course of treatment in the outpatient setting, however, has the drawback of the individual being continually exposed to gambling triggers. As gambling is normalised and highly accessible in our society, it increases the challenge for those in recovery from gambling addiction.

Some treatment programmes in Ireland offer an outpatient approach. This usually consists of seeing a psychiatrist, psychologist, or counsellor on a regular basis. The clinician coordinates and reviews the care plan of the patient over time. A care plan is an agreement between the clinician and the patient. It can be a written agreement that the patient signs. The professional will advise on the strategies most suited to the patient. The professional will also note any changes, both positive and negative over time, and advise the patient to make changes in their plan accordingly.

In recovery, many things can change from appointment to appointment. It is normal for cravings and mood to be very different each time the patient and professional meet. Similarly, anxiety levels, quality of sleep and energy levels can vary. A clinician can make an objective assessment of progress being made and relay positive feedback to the patient accordingly. It is sometimes the case that the patient is making considerable progress, although this may not be apparent to the patient themselves.

Many patients attend for professional review and are surprised to be told that they are making good progress when they themselves feel that they are static and not moving forward. The initial stages of recovery can be subtle, and while they may not be obvious to the patient or the people around them, they will be apparent to an experienced clinician. Helping individuals in recovery to be aware of their progress is a key feature of professional help. The more positive reinforcement an individual gets, the better they are going to do in the long run.

Outpatient input from a consultant psychiatrist

In the initial stages of caring for a patient with gambling addiction in the outpatient setting, I set appointments fortnightly or monthly. Occasionally, weekly appointments are required. As time goes on and as the patient improves, the severity of gambling disorder symptoms decrease and appointments become gradually less frequent. At this stage, appointments are every three to six months. After two years, I generally agree with the patient that it is time to refer back to their general practitioner.

I do not work alone in the outpatient setting. I also work closely with psychologists and counsellors. These professionals give me regular updates as to how the individual is doing. Outpatient treatment also involves co-ordinating a well-being programme for the individual. I might advise the patient to increase their exercise, attend pilates, start a yoga class, attend an evening course or start learning a new language. In addition, I will advise on attendance at mutual support meetings (see Chapter Five). I am also likely to advise on which mutual support meetings will be most beneficial in the area. We know from Chapter Five that mutual support meetings can vary greatly from meeting to meeting. Clinicians generally have a good idea of which meetings would be helpful for an individual.

A key role of the psychiatrist in the outpatient setting is to liaise with psychologists and counsellors when appropriate. A psychiatrist has initial training in medicine before completing postgraduate specialist training in psychiatry. A psychiatrist may prescribe medication, refer for psychology and counsellor input and advise lifestyle changes. Psychologists and counsellors provide various forms of therapy based on their training and areas of special interest. Psychologists have particular expertise in the provision of cognitive behavioural therapy for gambling disorder (see 'Psychological therapies' in this chapter). Mood problems are common, as are other mental health issues, during the course of recovery. Feeling down is part and parcel of gambling disorder recovery. Criticism from family members, debt problems and an inability to gamble anymore can all combine to leave the person thoroughly miserable. The question arises as to whether the person is depressed. In many cases the person is not depressed in a clinical sense but miserable in recovery. The term 'dysphoria' is often given to this state, whereby the person feels a persistent sense of being under the weather. The state does not reach the criteria needed for depression but is nevertheless problematic for the individual and the people around them. In some cases this dysphoria can tip into depression.

Depression occurs when the individual suffers from the lowering of mood with a loss of interest and a decrease in energy. This can be accompanied by a loss of appetite and sleep problems. Prescription of antidepressant medication, where there is a depressive illness, can make a huge difference to the well-being of the individual and makes recovery from gambling disorder much more likely. Cognitive behavioural therapy is also an effective treatment for depression.

Anxiety is also common in gambling disorder recovery. Recovery is challenging and involves a lot of change for the individual. This may mean taking on new roles within the family and at work. This is due to the fact that roles may have changed during the course of the addiction. If the individual was actively gambling, distraction and absenteeism may have been an issue. The person was possibly demoted or had a role altered. The individual suffering from gambling disorder may have lied in work saying that they were suffering stress or depression, when in fact they were gambling. The person may also have to navigate difficult relationship situations as a result of the damage gambling disorder has caused. All of this can conspire to leave the individual feeling unsure of themselves. For many, this is a temporary state which eases with time and reassurance. For others, it can become troubling to the extent that it starts impeding on everyday life and activities. As with the treatment of depression, the treatment of anxiety in gambling disorder with medication and/or cognitive behavioural therapy can be very helpful for the individual.

Addiction counselling

Whereas attendance at outpatient clinics with a specialist psychiatrist is likely to take place monthly or even less frequently, meeting with an addiction counsellor is usually much more frequent. Weekly attendance at one-to-one counselling for an hour allows an in-depth look at any issues arising in the previous week. Early recovery, in particular, can see many issues arising on a regular basis: emotions are running high and cravings can pose a particular problem. Family members are very worried and monitor the patient in a way that can feel smothering. Counsellors can have varied backgrounds in psychotherapy, addiction counselling and/or social work. The essence of good counselling hinges on having a good 'therapeutic alliance' with the patient.

Therapeutic alliance, or 'TA' as it is sometimes referred to, is the bond between the counsellor and the patient. Skilled counsellors form a strong TA easily. Counselling can have a major positive impact, not only on the individual but also on family members surrounding the individual. It is not unusual for clinical teams to refer family members for their own counselling. This may seem like overkill to the family member at first but is often appreciated as an invaluable input in due course. Family members are often at the epicentre of stress associated with trying to help the individual in active addiction, a process that is highly demanding.

All counsellors should be registered with a professional body such as the Addiction Counsellors of Ireland. Counselling, like all inputs in addiction recovery, should have a beginning, middle and end. Counselling should be finite, not open ended, whereby the individual has an opportunity to develop their own independence and stand on their own two feet. With this in mind, consideration should be given to discharging the person from counselling as soon as there is an opportunity to do so. It is not in the person's interest to develop a dependence on counselling.

That said, getting results in counselling takes time. It is impossible to put an exact time on how long counselling should last, with two years being a reasonable time for gambling disorder before the counsellor discharges the patient from their care. As time progresses, the frequency of meetings should decrease from an initial frequency of weekly to fortnightly, monthly and often three monthly in the second year of recovery.

Community-based inputs

Community addiction teams offer support to individuals and families affected by addiction including gambling disorder. The vast majority of this support is outpatient based. These services usually operate by self-referral. Once an individual makes contact with the service, an initial assessment appointment is made. Some community addiction teams offer a walk-in service where individuals can attend without any prior contact with the service. Some of the very effective community addiction teams offer a wide range of services – one-to-one addiction therapy, group therapy, a range of well-being therapies (yoga, mindfulness) and family support. Unfortunately, one's access to an effective community addiction team is dependent on location. An initial discussion with one's general practitioner is a good start to finding out more about what is available in a particular location.

Other community supports outside of community addiction teams are also available for gambling disorder. The Rise Foundation (therisefoundation.ie) offers outpatient input for individuals and families affected by addiction, including gambling disorder. Problem Gambling Ireland, headed up by addiction counsellor Barry Grant, offers a call-back service and experienced advice on gambling disorder treatment.

Psychological therapies

Cognitive behavioural therapy (CBT) is the psychological therapy most recommended for the treatment of gambling disorder. CBT is a short and focused psychological therapy delivered by qualified psychologists. The therapy is usually delivered over eight to twelve sessions, with each session lasting forty minutes to an hour. The therapy focuses on the 'here and now', rather than issues from the past.

Some psychologists will have a special interest in treating gambling disorder and it is wise to enquire about the particular psychologist's expertise in this area. CBT is effective for many but not all. As with all modalities of treatment in addiction, one has to try the input to see if it suits them. CBT is based on identifying faulty thinking patterns and promoting the use of more adaptive and constructive thinking strategies. Thoughts that lead to faulty thinking in CBT are called 'cognitive distortions'. Examples of cognitive distortions in gambling disorder are:

• **Magnification of gambling skill**

This occurs when one overrates one's gambling ability. It is the most apparent cognitive distortion in clinical services. Much of the poor decision-making in gambling disorder is based around the person's belief that they are highly skilled. Sometimes this also presents as an apparent arrogance where the person can continue to believe in their gambling expertise, even in the face of substantial losses. This can be infuriating for the person's loved ones.

- **Superstitious beliefs**

  Gambling has always been associated with superstitious practices. In non-disordered gambling, gamblers will have insight into the fact that the superstition may not have much grounds in reality. In gambling disorder, this insight can be lost with certain objects thought to bring good fortune. Examples of 'lucky charms' are ties, jewellery or hats but can be anything to which the individual attaches great significance. Disordered gamblers may also believe that certain actions will increase the probability of winning, such as kissing the dice, playing on certain slot machines, praying or singing.

- **Interpretative biases**

  Disordered gambling also presents with a number of cognitive distortions that fall under the category of 'biases'. These refer to the tendency to overestimate one's skill to explain wins and to underestimate the random nature of gambling. Gambler's fallacy is the belief that a series of losses will lead to a win. Euphoric recall is a tendency to selectively recall large wins and fail to recall the misery that came with disordered gambling.

- **Predictive skill**

  When gambling becomes increasingly chaotic, the decisions used to gamble can become random and even bizarre. Prompts to gamble can be bodily sensations, intuitions, feelings, omens, weather patterns, random events or even the particular day of the week.

The following case example shows how CBT can help to challenge and reconfigure the distorted thinking that is typical in gambling disorder.

CASE STUDY

CBT

Gary, twenty-nine, works in a financial firm in the city centre. He has struggled with gambling disorder for the past three years. He has persistently lied to his parents about needing money for various things. On one occasion he told them he was the victim of an online banking fraud; on another, that he fell foul of identity theft. More recently he told his parents he was mugged and a large sum of cash was stolen from him.

Eventually, his parents worked out he had a gambling problem when they saw a bank statement he left lying around. It contained hundreds of transactions with a betting company. In addition to Gary's lies, he also feels that he is particularly skilled at gambling. Although all the evidence suggests that he loses considerable amounts of money on a regular basis, he is unable to see this as he is suffering from an illness characterised by a lack of insight.

Gary also strongly believes that he is due a 'big win' as he has been on a losing run for quite a while. He frequently recalls the 'epic' days he had at race meetings many years ago. On these occasions he recalls the euphoria of picking the right horses on a number of occasions and the positive attention that he received as a result. He recalls the sense of superiority and elation that he felt as he strolled around the race course on these days.

The reality is that this was many years ago and happened on two occasions at most. On other occasions, he lost money and became quiet and irritable. Again, because Gary is suffering from a severe illness that affects his thinking, he is unable to identify his faulty thinking patterns and the damage they cause.

Gary's specialist referred him to a clinical psychologist for cognitive behavioural therapy. The first appointment consisted of an assessment, whereby the psychologist took an extensive history of Gary's gambling behaviours. A good deal of the focus was on his thinking patterns. The subsequent sessions identified many of Gary's 'cognitive distortions' or dysfunctional thinking patterns. He was assisted in becoming more proficient in identifying his dysfunctional thoughts by role playing some situations with the psychologist.

COMMENT

Moving on from this, with support he was able to identify particular situations where he might use more positive thinking. Over subsequent sessions and by practising between sessions, he became more aware of his faulty thinking. Although he still had strong and troubling cravings to gamble, he felt he had an additional tool within his armory to tackle them. He took part in ten sessions in total, at which point his psychologist performed a concluding assessment. This assessment revealed a significant reduction in the level of Gary's impaired thinking.

Medication

Naltrexone is a medication used in the treatment of gambling disorder. This is a drug called an opioid antagonist which works by blocking receptors in the brain called opioid receptors. This action has shown to affect the transmission of dopamine in the brain. Dopamine has long been thought to be involved in many reward processes in the body such as sex, eating and feeling elated.

Clinical trials have shown that naltrexone reduces the intensity of gambling urges. Our experience with the drug, like many drugs in medicine, is mixed. Some individuals respond really well to taking naltrexone, whereas others report no benefit at all. This reflects the trial and error nature of certain medications. Trial and error also applies with psychotherapy, with some individuals responding to psychological input and others not.

Naltrexone is a tablet prescribed at a starting dose of twenty-five milligrams. The dose can be increased to fifty milligrams, depending on the response to the medication. As part of prescribing naltrexone, the patient will be given information containing common and less common side effects. Common side effects are nausea, diarrhoea, stomach pain and cramping. Less common side effects are muscle pain and anxiety. The duration of taking naltrexone varies substantially. If there is no response to the drug, it is stopped. When naltrexone is effective, it can be continued for an indefinite period of time. When there are co-occuring psychiatric problems in gambling disorder, these can also be treated with appropriate medications. A common example is depression emerging during the course of gambling disorder treatment. In this instance, a treating doctor would consider prescribing an antidepressant. In other circumstances, there may be prominent anxiety symptoms where prescription of anti-anxiety medication is appropriate.

SUMMARY
- There are many different forms of professional help available for gambling disorder. Outpatient treatment usually includes attendance at mutual support meetings, one-to-one counselling and specialist psychiatric services.

Action plan for an individual affected by gambling disorder

1. Make an appointment with my general practitioner.
2. Ask my GP whether I should be referred to a consultant psychiatrist.
3. Seek out local Gamblers Anonymous and LifeRing meetings and consider attending.
4. Remove access to online gambling sites by self-excluding and/or installing gambling blocking software.
5. Self-exclude from local bookmakers.
6. Start engaging in well-being activities such as exercise, yoga and mindfulness.
7. Restrict access to all forms of funds – cash, credit and bank cards, credit union accounts. Recruit a family member/loved one to assist with this process. Consider transferring salary to family member.
8. Develop new hobbies or reactivate old ones.
9. Remember to reward myself after a period of not gambling.

10. Is there a community addiction team in my locality that offers services for gambling disorder? If so, call them and arrange an assessment appointment.

11. Consider cognitive behavioural therapy for gambling disorder with a qualified psychologist.

12. Organise one-to-one addiction counselling in my locality.

13. Consider medication with a consultant psychiatrist as a treatment option.

14. Call The Rise Foundation (therisefoundation.ie) to see are there free outpatient services available in my locality.

15. Call Problem Gambling Ireland (problemgambling.ie) to get further information and advice on the treatment of gambling disorder in Ireland.

Action plan for family members of an individual affected by gambling disorder

1. Attend general practitioner for advice on further steps.

2. Ask my GP whether my family member affected by gambling disorder should be referred to a consultant psychiatrist.

3. Seek out local Gam-Anon meetings and consider attending.

4. Consider one-to-one counselling with a counsellor experienced in dealing with the impact of gambling disorder on the family.

5. Consider assisting my family member with the management of funds – will I allow them to transfer their monthly salary to my account? Will I give them an agreed amount every day for spending?

6. Engage in self-care measures such as exercise, yoga and mindfulness.

7. Call The Rise Foundation to see if there are free outpatient services available in my locality.

8. Call Problem Gambling Ireland to get further information and advice on the treatment of gambling disorder in Ireland.

CHAPTER EIGHT
INPATIENT TREATMENT

Residential units dedicated to the treatment of gambling disorder are very rare. At the time of writing, there are no such units available in Ireland, with very few in the UK. This means that treatment for gambling disorder in the inpatient setting will entail participating in programmes where other addictions are also being treated. This reflects the situation with our own programme at St John of God Hospital where the majority of programme participants are in attendance for the treatment of alcohol and substance addictions. A common concern is that inpatient treatment may not be effective if the other participants are in treatment for addictions other than gambling disorder. We have largely found this not to be the case at our treatment facility. We find that the majority of individuals bond well with the others in the treatment programme and gain substantially from participation in the programme. Others will occasionally decide that the programme has no relevance to them at all and want to be discharged from the hospital. This, more often than not, reflects the ambivalence of the individual.

A major benefit of inpatient treatment is to provide the individual with time in a protected environment. In the outpatient setting, the individual is continuously exposed to gambling triggers and many opportunities to gamble. However, contrary to popular belief, the inpatient setting is not a panacea and does not provide total protection – if an individual is determined to gamble, even in a well-organised inpatient setting, they can unfortunately find ways to do so, such as asking other individuals who have access to a phone to gamble online on their behalf. Similarly, patients can ask those with access to betting shops to go out and place bets for them.

Inpatient programmes vary in length from twenty-eight days to five months and sometimes longer; most have aftercare programmes lasting from one to two years. The structure varies considerably with regard to time away. Our own programme offers weekend leave where the individual returns home three out of four weekends, from Friday through to Sunday evening. This is an important opportunity for the individual to put in place the wisdom gained during the course of the programme. It also prevents the possibility of the individual leaving the programme and facing a dramatic change in environment from the previous four weeks. Time in the inpatient setting also provides much needed breathing space for relatives. Up to the time of admission, there can be chaos and much worry among family members. At admission there can be a great sense of relief for the family that the patient is now in a safe place, away from further harm.

The philosophy of the treatment team in the inpatient setting is important as it defines the atmosphere of the facility. Our own unit promotes an environment of healing through non-confrontational means. This does not mean that patients are coming into the hospital for a holiday. It respects the fact that patients are suffering a medical illness and require support and care to get well. Patients need to be sure that they can trust the treatment team and that they will not be 'punished' or treated in a negative way. Relatives sometimes tell me that they had been researching the 'toughest' rehab they could find on the basis that the tougher the approach, the more likelihood of success. There is no evidence to support this.

Our philosophy is that success is achieved by building the patient's confidence through effective collaboration. Collaboration means that the patient drives their own recovery and feels in control of the process. Compassion is another central component in supporting individuals through gambling disorder recovery. Compassion should emanate from a sense that the individual is suffering from a condition that anyone could be affected by. Gambling disorder is a diagnosable brain disorder, characterised by deficits in key risk-processing areas of the brain. This illness should be treated like any other. When one attends for treatment of gambling disorder it should be the same as attending a general hospital for treatment of epilepsy, high blood pressure or diabetes. As gambling disorder is a relapsing remitting condition, compassion also needs to be applied in the case of frequent relapse. A feature of the illness, recognised by international bodies such as the World Health Organization, is relapse. It should not come as a surprise to anyone that relapse has occurred.

The continued accumulation of debt is one of the most destructive features of gambling disorder. Other addictions are also characterised by many forms of loss but usually not to the extent of that in gambling disorder. In the case of alcohol and drug addiction, money is spent on the substance, while time is lost consuming and recovering from the effects of the substance. Gambling disorder, as an illness, feeds on money. Without money, the illness cannot progress. Advice from debt management professionals in the inpatient setting can be very helpful as part of an overall plan of recovery. Multidisciplinary teams caring for patients with gambling disorder will ideally have access to debt managers. This, at present, is aspirational, however, as the vast majority of teams will not have access to any in-house debt management services. In our own centre, we refer patients to national debt agencies such as the Money Advice and Budgeting Service.

Many programmes offer support for families during the course of their programmes. In our own programme, we provide a day of support for family members or close friends on a fortnightly basis. Each programme has its own way of assisting families and has to find the way that works best for them. The family component varies in approach depending on the programme. Some programmes have a confrontational component. Others, such as our own, take a non-confrontational approach in the belief that confrontation does not help anyone, least so the patient. Our experience is that patients can become very anxious prior to the 'family day'. Patients catastrophise (expect the very worst) from the day. We do our best to convince participants that they will not be subject to a 'battering'. Sometimes these reassurances are in vain; however, more often than not the family day passes without problem for the patient. Families and close friends are very often key allies in recovery, so including them in treatment is essential.

In acute forms of gambling disorder, the inpatient setting provides an important place of safety from potential episodes of self-harm. As gambling disorder becomes more severe, the potential for self-harm increases. Some treatment centres, including our own, provide secure psychiatric facilities where intensive patient monitoring minimises the potential of a patient harming themselves. As we have noted, the reality in gambling disorder is that suicidal thoughts are not unusual and sometimes, unfortunately, patients can act on these thoughts.

Gambling disorder inpatient 'detox'

Following admission to the inpatient setting, the first concern is to provide the individual with time in a non-gambling environment. Prior to admission, the individual is caught in a spiral of compulsive loss chasing. All of the patient's being is obsessed with correcting a series of losses that they genuinely feel can be corrected. Some patients present with a sense of surrender and express a wish to refrain from gambling in the future. Others are not convinced that stopping gambling is necessary, but feel pressurised into treatment by relatives who overestimate the nature of the problem.

Mobile phone and computer use is not permitted in our inpatient setting to enable the patient to detach from compulsive device use. This can be a flashpoint, as not all patients agree with giving over their coveted devices. The reasons for taking away devices can be questioned and requests or even demands for exceptions to be made can follow. The treatment team has a responsibility to ensure that the environment is conducive to recovery for all. In this regard, it would make no sense to have exceptions to device usage in an environment of recovery. After the initial sense of annoyance, the majority of patients report a sense of relief and freedom from being away from their phone for a period of time. This effect is not limited to patients being treated for gambling disorder but also patients being treated for other addictions too.

This period of being unable to gamble represents a period similar to detoxing from alcohol or drugs, whereby the brain is allowed to start to heal. A block is put on the chaotic, destructive gambling that was occurring up to this point. Continued abstinence ensures the brain can continue to heal. Detox periods can vary depending on the needs of the patient. In some cases, the patient is motivated and determined to push forward to a rehabilitation treatment programme. In this case, the detox period might last one to two weeks. In other cases, the patient may be suffering co-existing mental health difficulties and require treatment for these problems. At other times, the patient's motivation to enter a rehab programme may not be optimal and the patient requires time to evaluate the reasons to proceed.

Inpatient rehab programmes

Following a detox period for gambling disorder, the next step for the person and their loved ones to consider is participation in a rehabilitation programme. For those who have health insurance, there are a number of centres nationally that offer such programmes. Most private programmes, including our own, offer rehabilitation over a twenty-eight-day period. Our own programme provides group and individual therapy combined with a range of well-being therapies which encourage the individual to consider new experiences. Very often participants tell me that they have no interest in pilates or feel mindfulness is of no use. Similarly, I am told that yoga is not for them. We deliberately deliver these well-being inputs to the programme to allow people to develop new interests. Much of recovery is about allowing new experiences and interests to develop and the inpatient setting is an ideal place for this to happen. Many patients report that they plan to continue these well-being inputs when they leave the inpatient programme. They also report that the inpatient programme helped them to become more open to new experiences and hobbies.

The inpatient setting also allows a concentration of therapy to occur within a short period of time. Group therapy usually occurs twice a day with an opportunity for one-to-one counselling in between. Participants of our programme may also attend Gamblers Anonymous during the course of the programme. For those who have not attended any groups prior to the programme, the inpatient setting is a great opportunity to build confidence within a group setting. Groups can be intimidating for many, especially in the early days of recovery. Inpatient programmes offer a means of being introduced to groups in a gentle and supported way with professionals facilitating the meetings.

After the inpatient programme and beyond

Many inpatient treatment programmes offer aftercare or what is called 'step-down' care. These programmes are generally a year long and consist of weekly or bi-weekly facilitated group therapy meetings. Within these programmes, protracted abstinence from gambling is the goal and participants should find pleasure in everyday activities increasing. A sense of well-being steadily increases to the point where the person starts to believe in the benefits of a gambling-free life. In the earlier stages of recovery, it is normal for the person to be taking part in recovery activities passively. Active recovery evolves over time. In active recovery, the person is motivated and fully engaged in getting well. Their behaviour suggests that they want to move away from gambling disorder and the problems that it previously caused. As time goes on, there are improvements in the individual's thinking. The level of preoccupation with gambling decreases and the faulty thinking that was prominent before recovery starts to improve. This leads to better decision making, particularly around risk processing. Similarly, there are improvements in mood and overall well-being. People speak of the relief of not being caught in a vortex of trying to organise money for ongoing gambling.

Trust builds with family and loved ones over time to the point where the person can resume previous responsibilities and roles within the family. Relationships heal and often revert to their pre-gambling addiction state. Very gradually, the person can increase the use of cash and credit facilities, even managing their own financial affairs. Similarly, transition from a non-smartphone back to a smartphone occurs as confidence grows around internet use. Attendance at mutual support meetings is generally reduced. Consultations with professionals continue outside of aftercare programmes but over time can reduce, with the ultimate goal of detaching from these services. Detaching from professional services is the high-water mark when it comes to recovering from gambling disorder.

The reality for some is that gambling disorder has led them into the criminal justice system. This may have meant a suspended sentence or worse, a period of incarceration. The person has to navigate life after such an apparently bleak set of circumstances. There is no questioning the potential impact of this on the individual but it does not need to define the individual's experience. I have worked with many individuals who have had to face the consequences of gambling disorder within the criminal justice system following a period of inpatient treatment. The good news is that people in these circumstances can, and generally do, move on.

For some, returning to an occupation where there is access to cash is not an option. An employer may have knowledge that the person has suffered from gambling disorder and will ensure that the person works in roles where there is no access to cash. For others, moving on from gambling disorder means a change of career and a change in direction away from a particular career. Some careers, particularly in finance, promote a preoccupation with money and have risk-taking as a feature.

During the course of an aftercare or step-down programme, relapse may occur, causing great pain and anguish for the individual and those around them. It can be very confusing for relatives when a loved one relapses after completing a period of intensive inpatient treatment. The central theme in supporting individuals during and after relapse is getting back to the care plan as promptly as possible. Much precious time can be spent catastrophising about the meaning of the relapse and questioning if it means that the patient is doomed. Clinical teams play a key role in supporting individuals to look at the big picture following relapse.

A key question arises as to the long-term effect of gambling disorder on close relationships, including marriages. Relationships are resilient in the face of the pressures of the illness and generally recover afterwards. The evidence suggests that families adapt, modify and maintain the family structure in the face of intense pressures. I frequently observe families and relationships being tested to their limit during the acute phases of gambling disorder. Wives or husbands of patients affected get all kinds of advice from other relatives on what to do in the situation. Sometimes there can be a strong push from relatives of a spouse affected to leave their partner. Sometimes couples do split up but, more often than not, they stay together and manage to salvage their relationship.

Recovery is also a time of great change. While one family member is suffering with gambling disorder, the family adapts and puts structures in place to cope. When in recovery, the family structure has to adapt back to the new structure. All of this involves change, and change, by its nature, is stressful. Families can and do manage this stress and move on to long-term recovery. Relatives learn to trust their loved one more over time as they gain more abstinence from gambling. Relatives may have been attending their own counselling and may decide to ease off or stop these sessions as their loved one gains more strength in recovery. Relatives say that the 'old version' of their loved one has returned and that it feels like 'having them back' from addiction.

When the individual is demonstrating protracted progress in aftercare or step-down programmes, relatives may decide to reduce the frequency of Gam-Anon sessions. Relatives usually reduce the input of their support structures according to what feels right for them. Alternatively, some relatives attend Gam-Anon for life. The level of checking and vigilance of the relative can also reduce to a point where they can get on with their own life without the constant fear that their loved one is engaging in destructive gambling.

SUMMARY
• Inpatient help offers an opportunity to remove oneself from gambling triggers in the community.

Inpatient treatment is not a viable option for everyone due to cost or time, in which case outpatient strategies become the main focus. Inpatient treatment programmes usually offer a combination of group and individual therapy.

USEFUL CONTACTS

The following list contains free services or resources for gambling addiction. The best place to start is by having a discussion with your general practitioner.

Mutual support
- Gamblers Anonymous: gamblersanonymous.ie
- Gam-Anon: gamblersanonymous.ie

Advice support
- Problem Gambling Ireland: problemgambling.ie

Outpatient treatment
- The Rise Foundation: therisefoundation.ie

Debt support
- Money Advice and Budgeting Service (MABS): mabs.ie

Dublin-based community addiction teams
- Dún Laoghaire Rathdown Community Addiction Team: dlrcat.ie
- Bray Community Addiction Team: bcat.ie

Information/contacts for local HSE addiction Services
- hse.ie/eng/services/list/5/addiction